WHAT
Every **K**indergarten
Teacher
Needs to Know

Margaret Berry Wilson

About
Setting Up
AND
Running a
Classroom

NORTHEAST FOUNDATION FOR CHILDREN, INC.

All net proceeds from the sale of this book support the work of Northeast Foundation for Children, Inc. (NEFC). NEFC, a not-for-profit educational organization, is the developer of the *Responsive Classroom*® approach to teaching, which fosters safe, challenging, and joyful elementary classrooms and schools.

The stories in this book are all based on real events in the classroom. However, to respect the privacy of students, their names and many identifying characteristics have been changed.

ISBN: 978-1-892989-44-4

Library of Congress Control Number: 2011933318

Cover and book design by Helen Merena.
Photographs by Jeff Woodward and Peter Wrenn. All rights reserved.

Thanks to the teachers and students of Garfield Elementary School, Springfield, Virginia; King Open School, Cambridge, Massachusetts; and Six to Six Magnet School, Bridgeport, Connecticut, who welcomed Northeast Foundation for Children to take photos in their classrooms.

Northeast Foundation for Children, Inc.
85 Avenue A, Suite 204
P.O. Box 718
Turners Falls, MA 01376-0718

800-360-6332
www.responsiveclassroom.org

15 14 13 12 11   7 6 5 4 3 2 1

CONTENTS

Knowing Kindergartners

There's something about kindergartners that makes teaching them a joy. Even the most sophisticated and worldly-wise kindergartner has a unique innocence and devotion to learning. I discovered this with pleasant surprise the first year I taught this grade. I will never forget the children's delight as the seeds they had planted sprouted into plants. Or their rapt attention as I read them stories. Or their intense concentration during a math lesson about telling time.

During the time lesson, I asked these eager students to look at the clock and say what they noticed—they took the assignment so seriously, pointing out things that after forty-plus years of life I had never much noticed. ("I noticed that the second hand kind of gets stuck every time it passes the minute hand, but only really fast!" "I noticed that the minute hand doesn't point straight to the dot!") They were equally observant during other "noticings," and so happy about every new book, theme, letter, math concept, and science project.

Kindergartners can soak in so much information and learn skills so quickly. One kindergartner I taught began school knowing no alphabet letters, being able to count only to ten, and knowing no one in our class. Two months later, she knew all of her letters and sounds, could count to fifty, and had befriended many classmates. By midyear, she was reading simple books, decoding CVC (consonant-vowel-consonant) words, such as *cat* and *dog*, adding and subtracting simple numbers, and acting as a classroom leader! Although her trajectory was a bit extraordinary, most kindergartners do make rapid and rewarding progress during the year.

Of course, kindergartners don't make these leaps and bounds all on their own. In fact, they need a special kind of adult support and guidance. With

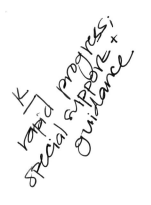

their literal interpretation of the world, unfamiliarity with school culture, and dependence upon adults, kindergartners need highly skilled and loving teachers. They benefit from teachers who plan activities that are concrete and interactive, give clear directions, and are well prepared to react calmly—to anything that might come up. These teaching skills help children of all ages, but they are critical for teaching kindergartners effectively.

I actually thought I was pretty strong in these areas . . . and then I was moved from second grade to kindergarten. This happened during the school year with only a weekend's notice. I didn't have time to research what to expect, and my first days of teaching kindergarten showed it—those days were challenging both for the children and for me.

I gave the children too many directions and was frustrated when they didn't follow through. I was unprepared for the avalanche of children leaving their seats during work time to ask me, "Should I use blue here?" or "Can I go to the bathroom?" I was taken aback when a few kindergartners cried at what I considered minor setbacks (in second grade, crying usually indicated a more serious issue). And I was surprised when some children did not know how to use materials that I considered basic for this age group. But once I learned more about kindergartners and how to give them what they needed, I discovered how rewarding teaching this grade can be.

I wrote this book to help you get off to a good start teaching kindergarten. In it, I provide you with some ways to build upon kindergartners' strengths while also helping them overcome some of their challenges. For instance, I address how to schedule a kindergarten day (or half day), how to help kindergartners adjust to school and form a bond with you and their classmates, and how to successfully work with kindergarten parents. The book will help you whether you're new to teaching or have taught kindergarten before. Enjoy the journey!

⬤ ⬤ ⬤ ⬤ ⬤ ⬤

Once I learned more about kindergartners
and how to give them what they needed, I discovered
how rewarding teaching this grade can be.

Understanding Children's Development

As I learned when I took on my first kindergarten class, all teachers, even those with experience in other grades, need to understand and appreciate what is unique about each particular grade, especially kindergarten. Although each kindergartner is of course an individual, many share some general developmental characteristics. Knowing these general traits and abilities can give you a starting point for setting up developmentally appropriate routines and transitions—and thus better support children for success.

In my first year with kindergartners, learning more about their common language and cognitive characteristics helped me to more effectively structure lessons and classroom routines. Realizing how important it is to use concrete and basic language with many kindergartners led me to plan more carefully the vocabulary I used in giving directions, leading transitions, and teaching lessons. For instance, I often taught games involving making or getting "pairs" of cards. After some initial confusion, I discovered that some students (many of whom were also English language learners) didn't know what "a pair" was or thought I was asking them to somehow make fruit out of their cards!

As I started to look at words through kindergarten eyes, I brought in more actual objects and photos of objects to illustrate new or different concepts. I learned to connect new material more concretely to what children already knew or had only recently learned.

Discovering kindergartners' need for and love of repetition, I also tried to build in rhymes, repeat favorite activities, and use predictable structures in my lessons. For instance, I taught the children how to play concentration with a partner and then used that same game structure to review many concepts we had learned. Repetition helps build kindergartners' competence and confidence, enabling them to gradually try out new and different ways of completing learning tasks and activities. By providing repetition throughout the school day and year—in songs, games, routines, and so on—I was addressing a critical developmental need of kindergartners.

I also learned to break down routines into smaller parts and teach each part separately. To teach behavior expectations for when we met as a whole group in the circle area, I first thought about how to define each child's

3

basic & concrete language i.e. do they know what "pairs" are?

repetition

space. Even though I inherited a rug with pre-marked spaces for where children should sit in the circle, I discovered that the class still benefited from my pointing out these spaces and how to know the boundaries for each.

Then I taught students how to check to make sure they were in their own space and how to respectfully let others know when they felt encroached upon. (To teach these and other skills, I use a teaching method called interactive modeling, which is described in detail in Chapter 2, "Schedules and Routines," starting on page 43.) Because young children usually don't know where to put their hands and legs when sitting in the circle, I modeled how to do this as well.

Although with older students I often gave choices about how to sit, I found that kindergartners did better with one clear set of expectations and far fewer choices. Other "circle" behaviors that I broke down and taught included how to show attentive listening, how to signal a need to go to the bathroom, and how to signal a desire to contribute to a conversation. By understanding children's common developmental characteristics, I was better able to tailor my teaching of these and other routines to help set kindergartners up for success in school.

Common Characteristics of Kindergartners

The table on pages 6–7 summarizes some common characteristics of children in this grade. Knowing these characteristics can help you plan and tailor your teaching, set up the classroom, and work with parents, all to best meet kinder-gartners' needs. As you use this table to help you in your teaching, keep these points in mind:

■ Human development is complex. Even scientists who study it do not yet fully agree on the means by which humans grow socially, emotionally, linguistically, or cognitively. Most theorists describe the process as involving a dynamic interaction between a person's biological disposition and many other environmental factors—including the historical era in which a person grows up, the person's culture and family, and the institutions he or she encounters (such as schools, places of worship, and the media). The table is not intended to ignore this complexity, but rather to offer you a bridge between the abstract ideas of theory and their practical expression in children's classroom behavior.

- ■ **Every child is unique.** As a result of the complex and dynamic process of development, no two children—not even identical twins with the same genetic makeup—will develop in the same way or at the same rate. Also, within a given child, one area may develop at a much faster rate than another. For example, a kindergartner might have moved past the literal and concrete phase in language development but still struggle with simple gross motor actions such as running and jumping.

- ■ **The table gives you a practical frame of reference.** Sometimes when we see certain behaviors or behavior patterns in classrooms, we wonder: "What's going on here?" "Is it me or something I'm doing that's causing this?" "Is there something more I should know about this child or these children?" The table will give you a place to turn to if you're wondering about a behavior, whether you should address it, and, if so, how. For example, as the table shows, many kindergartners seek frequent feedback from adults. As we help these children build self-confidence and a sense of competence so that they become less dependent on their teacher's opinion, it's helpful to know that needing frequent adult approval is a fairly common stage in kindergartners' development.

In brief, this table is not intended to limit your thinking about kindergartners' potential or to lead you to ignore the needs of children who differ from other kindergartners. For example, although many kindergartners like to please their teachers and follow the rules, not all will. Don't assume that something is "wrong" with children who test limits more. Instead, figure out how to give them the boundaries and guidance they need. Think of the table not as an ending point, but as a starting point.

To learn more about child development, see the resources in the "About Child Development" section on pages 148–149.

5

Kindergartners

Common Characteristics	School Implications

Social-Emotional

- Need a great deal of adult approval—like to know exactly what's expected and that they're meeting those expectations.

- Enjoy helping and following the rules.

- Like to ask for and receive permission.

- Often have difficulty seeing things from another person's point of view. Tend to think there's only one "right way."

- Enjoy routines and structure.

- Often cry when upset, embarrassed, angry, or confused.

- Give frequent positive and specific reinforcement to all children, including when they accomplish tasks independently.

- Check in with children frequently to make sure they understand directions.

- Try to have predictable schedules and routines.

- Use children's literature, drama, role-play, and other strategies to help kindergartners develop a repertoire of social skills (for example, what to do when they're upset, how to put themselves in someone else's shoes, how to explore alternative ways of doing something, and how to monitor their own work).

Physical

- Focus best visually on objects or writing that is close to them.

- Are better at gross motor tasks (such as running and jumping) than at earlier ages, but still can be awkward with small motor movements.

- May find printing challenging—for instance, they may reverse certain letters or numbers.

- Are very active and energetic.

- Are prone to falling out of chairs, often sideways.

- Avoid having children copy from the board or from a chart placed far away from them.

- Provide frequent movement breaks and include movement in daily lessons and routines.

- Give children regular opportunities for recess and physical play.

- Provide scaffolding for fine motor tasks, especially printing. Place dots on the paper to show where to start writing or give children a craft stick (or remind them to use their finger) to help them space between words.

Kindergartners

Common Characteristics	School Implications

Cognitive

- Like to repeat experiences and copy previous products.
- Often have difficulty seeing more than one way to do something.
- Can pace themselves and work quietly for longer periods of time (eventually up to fifteen or twenty minutes), but will generally need teacher approval and support to change activities.
- Like to learn through direct experience or hands-on learning.

- Provide learning experiences that are mostly active and interactive, and include repetition.
- Reinforce their efforts, but gently nudge them into trying new things and reassure them that mistakes are okay.
- Provide a few models for how to do assignments beforehand and allow for frequent sharing of their work.
- Check in with children briefly before expecting them to change activities.

Language

- Are often very literal and basic in their understanding of language.
- Express themselves briefly—sometimes in just a few words.
- Often think out loud (for example, saying "I'm going to choose the black crayon" before taking the black crayon).

- Think through (and sometimes even write out for yourself) your directions and explanations in advance. Display class rules, key routines, and schedules, and choral-read them.
- Break assignments and tasks into easily understood and manageable parts. Expect and allow quiet talking during work time.
- Check in frequently and assess children's understanding.
- Avoid overreacting to impulsive statements. Instead, guide children to think before speaking (for example, teach them to wait a few seconds before responding).

7

The information in this chart is based on *Yardsticks: Children in the Classroom Ages 4–14*, 3rd ed., by Chip Wood (Northeast Foundation for Children, 2007), and is consistent with the following sources:

Child Development Guide by the Center for Development of Human Services, SUNY, Buffalo State College. 2002. WWW.BSC-CDHS.ORG/ FOSTERPARENTTRAINING/PDFS/CHILDDEVELGUIDE.PDF

"The Child in the Elementary School" by Frederick C. Howe, *Child Study Journal*, Vol. 23, Issue 4. 1993.

Your Child: Emotional, Behavioral, and Cognitive Development from Birth through Preadolescence by AACAP (American Academy of Child and Adolescent Psychiatry) and David Pruitt, MD. Harper Paperbacks. 2000.

What about Developmentally Younger and Older Kindergartners?

Schools and school systems have different cutoff dates for when children can begin kindergarten, so you may have students who are younger or older than what is typically considered kindergarten age. Even within a group of children who are approximately the same chronological age, some will likely have developmental traits more typical of older or younger children.

Chronologically or developmentally younger kindergartners may demonstrate behaviors more often associated with preschoolers. Consider the following common characteristics of younger kindergartners and the accompanying ideas for how you can adapt your teaching accordingly:

■ **Often clumsy and able to sit still for only short periods of time.** Avoid jumping to the conclusion that these children have attentional issues. While some might, many others may just be going through a phase of development. Try to modify or scaffold physical tasks for them—for example, have them serve the nonliquid portions of snack, or make pathways in the classroom more visible for them so that they do not step on other children as they move around. Explore ways to make their work periods shorter—for example, shorten their assignments or let them do a quick check-in to show you or a classmate their work halfway through a work period. Provide lots of physical activity breaks and a variety of hands-on explorations.

■ **Love talking and being with friends, but often engage in more parallel (rather than interactive) play and dialogue.** Build in frequent opportunities for these children to talk during instructional and independent work times. At independent work times, seat children who share this parallel play characteristic together and somewhat separate from peers who might prefer a little more quiet. Follow up with these children when they don't

Clumsy & short attention spans

immediately crying when blamed for something or in trouble

respond to you or classmates: "Jeremy, Jena asked if you wanted to swing on the swings with her. Go ahead and tell her 'yes' or 'no, thank you.'"

■ **May respond physically when upset and need adult assistance to express emotions verbally.** Look for these children's "triggers" and try to head off physical responses. Respond with firmness and respect when a student is becoming upset—for example: "Marissa, stop. Take a breath. Walk to me." If a child hits or hurts another, give a clear and firm logical consequence. For example: Begin with a time-out and then consider moving the child to another spot to work (if the hitting occurred during a work time). Devote some class time to doing role-plays, reading stories, and reflecting on ways children can calm down and let people know in a respectful way when they're angry or upset.

Some of your kindergartners may be chronologically or developmentally older—with traits more typical of first graders. Here are some of the common characteristics and ideas for how to adjust your teaching to support these children:

9

■ **Highly social and energetic.** Provide lots of noncompetitive, cooperative activities that will give these children a chance to move and socialize in positive ways. As with younger kindergartners, limit the times when you require these children to be quiet. When possible, group them with other children who need to talk some as they work.

■ **Often in a hurry and excited to learn, but not too concerned about creating a perfect product.** Reinforce their efforts and understand that they'll grow into caring more about their finished products. For instance, if a child brings you a picture that is sketchily drawn, with few details, ask him or her to tell you about it. Often, children see more in their work than we can. Your

Ask students to "explain your thoughts"

listening will show your respect and help you more accurately gauge their learning.

■ **Talkative and enjoy explaining their thoughts.** Provide many opportunities for children to explain how something happened and how things work. Try to check in with them several times a day for a quick chat. Doing so will help reduce how often they need to seek you out.

How to Use This Book

You can use this book in various ways. For example:

■ **Read cover to cover.** This book is intended to walk you through setting up and running an effective kindergarten classroom. So if you know far enough in advance that kindergarten will be your assigned grade, read the whole book straight through.

■ **Right now all I want to know is . . .** If, like me, you find out that you're teaching kindergarten with little advance notice, just read the sections that are the most pertinent or interesting to you at first. Maybe you want to make sure you get off to a good start with parents. Go right to Chapter 5, "Communicating with Parents," starting on page 111. Or maybe you want to make sure you break up routines into tiny steps and teach those thoroughly. If so, head right to Chapter 2, "Schedules and Routines," starting on page 37. Read what you need and then return to the other chapters when you have more time.

No matter which path you choose, be careful not to let yourself get overwhelmed while you read. Try a few strategies or ideas at a time when you're ready for them. Come back to the book for more information as you gain confidence in your kindergarten teaching abilities. Don't worry if you're not doing everything at first—no one is! Also, try not to worry too much about making mistakes as you teach. The struggle and beauty of teaching is that you can always improve. Your students will continue to learn as you make adjustments and fine-tunings, and they can greatly benefit from seeing a real-life model of an adult who is a lifelong learner.

10

Last Word

On the last day of my second year teaching kindergarten, I shared the news that I was going to have a baby boy. The children's questions and advice told me a great deal about what they were taking away from kindergarten: "Are you going to teach him all the songs you taught us?" "Are you going to read him some good books like you read us?" "Are you going to let him win games?" "You're going to need to be firm with him sometimes!"

With kindergartners so excited about learning and so open, you can make a positive difference in their lives. You can help them feel excited about school and what it has to offer. You can foster social and academic skills and qualities, such as persistence, resiliency, assertion, and cooperation, that they'll need for school success. I hope this book helps you do these things (and more) in practical and inspiring ways. What you say and do as a kindergarten teacher truly matters!

help Kindergart. feel excited about school!

CHAPTER 1

Classroom Setup

As I write this book, I am also redecorating my little boy's room, changing it from the baby version I did before he was born to one that suits who he is and what he needs now as a two-year-old. I see that his baby room was all about me—from my favorite shade of pale yellow to the amazing "Hey, Diddle, Diddle" curtains and quilt that my mom and aunt made. It's the room *I* dreamed about.

You may have an idea for the kindergarten classroom that you've dreamed about, too. Perusing teacher catalogs, you can find all sorts of adorable furniture, kits to cover all sorts of curriculum concepts, and stuffed animals of all sizes. But if you get too carried away with your dream, you could end up with a room that is overstimulating for kindergartners. Or, when you work on your curriculum, you may discover that the supplies you've gathered don't really support your lesson plans. Perhaps you'll want to add bulletin boards to display children's work but realize that your walls are already full. The room may fulfill your dream, but will it serve the real needs of children in the classroom and your actual teaching?

Think preparation, not decoration. What kindergartners need is a simple, warm, and inviting classroom. The furniture should be minimal and functional, arranged to support how children will be working; the room organized so that they can easily find what they need and explore subject areas in a calm and hands-on way. They need a room that feels as if it is theirs, with their creations exhibited on the walls, with their favorite songs and poems displayed, and with books they enjoy neatly placed on shelves.

This chapter will help you set up a kindergarten classroom while always keeping the children in mind. It covers how to arrange the furniture; use, store, and organize supplies; and design classroom displays that serve a learning purpose.

13

Arranging the Furniture

Whole-Group Circle

For me, it would be nearly impossible to teach kindergarten without an adequate and inviting circle space. The circle is important in all elementary grades, but especially vital in kindergarten. The circle provides a sense of togetherness for kindergartners. It helps them develop a greater ability to understand other points of view. It also provides an open space for the active and interactive learning that kindergartners need—hands-on, social, engaging, and appropriately paced.

The circle is especially helpful in getting every school day off to a great start. Having the children come together first thing each morning to greet each other, laugh, sing, and share can make such a difference. It can help those who had a rough start at home put that behind them, help those who are still feeling a little unsure in the class feel more secure, and help everyone feel more invested in supporting each other. For my own morning kindergarten gatherings, I use the *Responsive Classroom*® Morning Meeting structure. But whichever structure you use, children will benefit from a well-designed circle space.

Learn More about Morning Meeting at
www.responsiveclassroom.org

The Morning Meeting Book by Roxann Kriete (Northeast Foundation for Children, 2002).

"Morning Meeting: A Powerful Way to Begin the Day," *Responsive Classroom Newsletter*, February 1999.

Ways to Use the Circle

Curriculum Area	Use the Circle for . . .
Social	Class meetings, practicing social skills and routines, singing, group games and activities
Writing	Mini-lessons, work sharing, interactive writing
Reading	Read-alouds; partner chats about books, poetry, and other shared reading experiences; dramatizations of books; mini-lessons about reading strategies; independent reading
Math	Explorations of manipulatives, mini-lessons, math games
Social studies	Read-alouds, examination of artifacts, dramatizations of historical events
Science	Read-alouds, examination of materials, experiments and other hands-on activities

You can also use the circle for instruction (see "Ways to Use the Circle" above). Plus, you can have children return to the circle whenever they need a movement break. Or have them work on the floor of the circle if they're not yet comfortable working at a table.

The circle is so important to teaching and children's learning that I plan this space first every year. Here are my recommendations for how to set up a circle area:

■ **Use a large space.** Kindergartners thrive on active learning, so allow enough room for movement, active games, dramatizations, and similar activities. Ideally, each kindergartner will have enough room to stand up and move in her own spot (and not land in a neighbor's lap if she falls over sideways, which sometimes happens!). Also, allow enough space in the circle area for a chart stand and any other supplies you plan to use for whole-group instruction. Consider using a rug or carpet squares for more comfortable seating on the floor.

■ **Try to make a true circle.** A circle works best when everyone can see each other and when every child can see the chart stand or easel. An actual circle, as opposed to a square or other shape, helps ensure these results. It can also discourage unwanted behavior, such as children shifting around to make themselves the center of attention or to hide from view.

■ **Mark spots.** Kindergartners do best when they know exactly where to sit in the circle. There are many commercially made rugs with spots marked. However, a more economical solution is to mark spots with removable tape or tape numbers, letters, or index cards (possibly with a photo) at each spot.

■ **Assign circle seats.** To ease transitions to and from the circle and keep the focus on learning, assign each child a seat. Without assigned seats, you may end up with some children vying to sit next to you or a favored friend while others try to sit farther away from you than you might like.

■ **Rotate seat assignments.** You also want kindergartners to have a chance to interact with a variety of classmates. Help them accomplish this by changing their circle seats every week or two.

■ **Move children as needed.** Be flexible and set children up for success by switching assigned spots sooner than planned if the need arises. For example, if two children sitting next to each other find it hard to refrain from talking or are having conflicts, assign them new seats immediately to ensure that circle time stays positive and productive.

16

If Your Room Is Small

If your room is tight, be creative in finding space for a circle and resist the urge to give up on it. See if you can save space in other areas of the room (see "Three Pieces of Furniture You Can Lose" below). At least, try to set up the classroom so that you can meet as a whole group (with space for children to move around), even if the space can't be a circle.

Three Pieces of Furniture You Can Lose

■ **A teacher's desk.** These often take up a great deal of space, but we seldom use them to teach. When I got rid of my desk, I had many more options for arranging the classroom and collected much less clutter.

■ **A large file cabinet.** These encourage us to keep things we don't need. Think smaller. What files are essential? You can probably store these in one or two mobile file cabinets.

■ **The latest, greatest thing.** Education has fads, and furniture is no exception. My first year of teaching, I paid too much for a nifty folding table to house the listening center. The table never really worked and always seemed to be in the way. You're better off sticking to the basics.

Work Tables

Kindergartners need space to do independent, partner, and small-group work. If you can, have children work at tables rather than desks and put needed supplies on the tables (or nearby). Tables can offer more actual work space and greater flexibility than desks—you can use tables for both independent work and center areas.

If you use desks, arrange them in small groups, such as groups of four, and avoid front-facing rows. Also avoid having kindergartners use desk storage spaces because keeping desk contents organized can prove quite a struggle for them. If possible, arrange the desks so that the storage spaces are inaccessible.

■ **Assign seats for some parts of the day.** When children need to work on one independent task, such as writing workshop, assign seats at tables or other work areas. Knowing exactly where to go to work will make transitions from one area to another smoother for children.

■ **Change seat assignments frequently.** Kindergartners need help getting to know their classmates and learning how to interact with a wide variety of friends. Rotate seat assignments every two to four weeks to provide them with these opportunities.

■ **Offer alternative spaces.** Although most kindergartners can work productively at tables with others around them, some may prefer more isolated spaces at times. Scatter a few desks around the room. If you can't do this, provide children with clipboards or lap desks. Use interactive modeling to show children how to move to alternate work spaces and how to use clipboards or lap desks. (See Chapter 2, "Schedules and Routines," pages 43–51, for more on interactive modeling.) Explain that once they move to a non-table spot, they need to stay there—and practice what this looks like with them ahead of time.

> **Tips for Assigning Table Spots or Desk Seats**
>
> ■ Balance the number of boys and girls in each group, if possible. Make sure all children eventually sit with everyone in the class.
>
> ■ Group children strategically. For example, group children who have been working well together with each other. Group children who need lots of quiet together.
>
> ■ Do some children need a little extra help at work time? Have them sit with classmates who are able to help them (without being distracted from their own work).

students who need help sitting w/ those who can help them.

17

(handwritten, in left margin) Tables double as center areas

18

■ **Set up tables as "center areas" if you plan to have centers or choice time.** Tables can double as center areas if you place bookshelves with needed supplies for the centers nearby. For instance, put one table and a shelf of art supplies near the sink to serve as an art center. Another table could serve as a math center, with manipulatives nearby, and so on.

Other Areas of the Classroom

Although it's a good idea to keep furniture and other materials to a minimum, you may find that you need a few additional areas and furnishings. When planning these, remember that you should be able to see every child (and every child should be able to see you) from all areas of the room, so choose furniture that is no taller than your average kindergartner.

■ **A multifunctional table area.** Plan an area that enables you to work with small groups or with individual children on reading, writing, and math. A table big enough to seat you and several children would work, as would a small area rug.

■ **A classroom library.** Kindergartners need a variety of books to read or look at on their own. The classroom library should also contain a variety of books for the class as a whole, including those for read-alouds.

If you have space, store books within easy reach of the children and use front-facing baskets so that they can flip through and see the covers as they browse. Use bookshelves that are low enough for children to see the books on each shelf and for you to see the children while they're in the library. If your school allows it, include beanbag chairs, pillows, and reading lights to make a cozy reading area. (See "The Classroom Library" on page 26 for more on classroom library books.)

- **An active play area.** Plan an area or areas where children can move and build with blocks, work on puzzles, engage in dramatic play, and enjoy other activities. If space is limited, this area could also be used as the circle area.

- **A computer area.** If you have classroom computers, keep them apart from other areas and centers so that you can easily monitor children's computer use. If this is impractical because of space considerations, turn off and cover computers when not in use.

Classroom Supplies

I think of kindergarten as an experimental year during which children get to try out many materials and develop a repertoire of skills for how to use them. Kindergartners need a wide variety of high-quality equipment and supplies to maximize their active and interactive learning. But be careful not to overdo it—if the room is cluttered with too much stuff, children may feel overwhelmed and end up being less careful than you would like. Follow these guidelines for acquiring supplies and helping children use and care for them.

> **Seeking Supplies**
>
> In addition to asking parents to contribute supplies, explore using a website set up to link interested donors with classrooms. For example:
>
> - WWW.DONORSCHOOSE.ORG
> - WWW.ILOVESCHOOLS.COM
> - WWW.ADOPTACLASSROOM.ORG

Have Community Supplies Only

The traditional approach to supplies is to give families a list of items to purchase for their individual child. Problems can arise with this approach, however. For example, children may be envious of a classmate's special pen or superhero folder. Also, some families may not be able to afford supplies or have time to shop for a long list of items.

Instead of this traditional approach, try a community supplies approach in which each parent donates one category of supplies to the class (one parent supplies the pencils, another some markers, and so forth). Or provide all the supplies yourself (if you have a supply budget). Either way, the community supplies approach creates a sense of fairness and equity in the classroom: All the children will have what they need and can share equally.

Using community supplies also gives children the opportunity to try out different kinds of supplies and figure out what works best for them. Finally, having one set of supplies creates a sense of shared ownership in the classroom, which in turn contributes to a sense of common purpose and community.

Despite all the good reasons for having community supplies, many parents may not be used to this approach. Be sure to share your reasons for choosing it when you ask them to purchase things.

What Supplies Do Kindergartners Need?

Kindergartners need a lot of stuff, so it's easy to get overwhelmed when you start assembling supplies. Try to prioritize—start with what's most essential. Then add to what you have by seeking donations from other teachers and families, looking for sales, and using other money-saving strategies. The tables below and on the next three pages make a great starting point in prioritizing supplies for a kindergarten class.

Dealing With What You Inherit

If you inherit supplies when you begin teaching kindergarten, you may find it hard to decide what to keep. Here are some "toss" guidelines:

- **Out-of-date materials.** Rarely is there any reason to keep old textbooks or unused workbooks from prior curriculum adoptions. Instead, offer them to interested families or return them to the central office.

- **Materials with missing parts, or things you just don't like.** If you can salvage something useful (game tokens, for instance), do so. Otherwise, get rid of these materials! If you don't like them now, you won't use them later.

- **Mystery materials.** If you don't know what something is or how to use it, ask more experienced colleagues for their advice about whether it's worth keeping.

Good Supplies for a Kindergarten Classroom

Category	Early in the Year	Later in the Year	Sample Quantities
Literacy	■ Books (variety of genres and levels) ■ Chart paper and stand; pocket chart ■ Pointers for reading charts and big books ■ Listening center and audio books ■ Variety of paper ■ Pencils, erasers, felt tip pens, grips ■ Writing notebooks, journals, or folders ■ Magnetic letters and cookie sheets ■ Puppets and finger puppets ■ Letter stamps and stamp pads ■ Letter stencils	■ Books (new genres and authors as replacements) ■ Bookmaking supplies (cardstock, hole punchers, yarn, etc.) ■ Small dry erase boards, nontoxic dry erase markers, and erasers ■ Envelopes	■ Pencils—about eight per child ■ Pencil grips—about two per child ■ Magnetic letters and cookie sheets—enough for a group of four or five children
Music	■ Variety of CDs or downloaded music ■ Charts of songs ■ Rhythm sticks ■ Maracas, bells, other hand instruments	■ Additional CDs and downloaded music	■ Two rhythm sticks per child ■ One hand instrument per child

21

CONTINUED

Category	Early in the Year	Later in the Year	Sample Quantities
Math	■ Counters ■ Unifix cubes ■ Pattern blocks ■ Unit blocks ■ Rulers, meter sticks, tape measures ■ Math games ■ Dice or spinners ■ Playing and numeral cards ■ Tactile numbers and shapes ■ Materials and trays for sorting ■ Real or play coins	■ Pattern block cards ■ Tangrams ■ Geoblocks ■ New math games ■ Play clock with movable hands ■ Attribute blocks ■ Stamps and stamp pads ■ Dominoes ■ Calculators	■ Pattern blocks, Unifix cubes, etc.—several sets ■ Counters—several different sets ■ Playing and numeral cards—one set of each for every two children
Social Studies	■ Globe ■ Maps, especially of school and local area	■ Map puzzles ■ Theme-related artifacts, posters, etc.	■ One globe per class ■ Several maps of different types
Choice Time and Recess (outdoor and indoor)	■ Variety of balls ■ Cones to mark areas ■ Hula hoops ■ Jump ropes ■ Sidewalk chalk ■ Blocks ■ Board games ■ Legos, puzzles ■ Small animal toys ■ Small cars, trucks, and other vehicles	■ More complex games ■ More complex puzzles	■ Three to four balls per class ■ Four to six single jump ropes and two longer ones

Good Supplies for a Kindergarten Classroom

Category	Early in the Year	Later in the Year	Sample Quantities
Art	■ Crayons ■ Colored pencils ■ Markers (thin and thick) ■ Paint, paint cups, brushes, and easels; smocks or old T-shirts ■ Drawing paper ■ Construction paper ■ Magazines for cutting ■ Brown paper bags ■ Collage materials (buttons, fabric, cotton balls, etc.) ■ Scissors ■ Glue and glue sticks ■ Tape ■ Modeling clay ■ Craft sticks	■ Watercolors and brushes ■ Small trays for paint (ask at your local grocery store if you can have some for free) ■ Colored tissue paper ■ Yarn ■ Glitter ■ Toothpicks ■ Hole punch ■ Scissors with decorative edges ■ Origami paper ■ Stamps and stamp pads ■ Staplers	■ Scissors—one pair for every child ■ Glue—one bottle for every two children ■ Glue sticks—two per child ■ Markers, crayons, colored pencils—an ample supply for each table cluster ■ Yarn, glitter, other specialty supplies (bring out less often)
Science	■ Hand lenses ■ Small trays ■ Seeds, beans, shells, rocks, polished stones, and similar natural objects ■ Magnets	■ Balance scales ■ Containers for growing things or observing living things ■ Theme-related artifacts, pictures, and posters	■ Hand lens—one for each child ■ Small tray—at least one per child ■ Balance scale—one or two at a center

See the appendix (pages 137–141) for favorite books, board games, and websites for kindergartners.

Quality of Supplies Matters

Much like adults, kindergartners are better able to do their best work when they have high-quality materials at hand. That doesn't mean everything has to be new—for example, I actually prefer older pattern blocks to newer ones because the wood has a heftier feel and texture—but materials must be well cared for and in good working order.

When purchasing new supplies, choose those of high quality. Because quality varies widely, specify the brands you trust when communicating supply needs to parents and other donors. Or ask experienced colleagues for their recommendations. Then, so that supplies will last, be vigilant about how children care for them. Finally, set aside time now and then to cull through supplies and get rid of anything that's not in good shape.

Storing and Organizing Supplies

Use an organizational system that will make sense for both you and the children. Here are some tips:

■ **Have student cubbies.** Although kindergartners do best without desks, they still need a space for coats, sweaters, backpacks, papers, folders, and notes that go back and forth between home and school. If you can, have cubbies (or a basket or shelf) in the classroom for each child so that you can keep your eye on children as they put things away or retrieve needed materials.

■ **Set up a storage system for folders that stay at school.** Depending on the curricular approach you use, children may have writing folders, math and science journals, and other collections of work. You may need to review these frequently while giving children easy access to them, too. One storage system that works well is using small, hanging file holders for student folders and crates for hardbound journals. Organize folders and journals in alphabetic order or by group designations so that they can be found quickly and easily. Also helpful is having groups of folders and journals split up into different areas of the room for easier access.

- **Put close-at-hand supplies on tables.** You'll want children to have easy access to some supplies (such as pencils, erasers, and crayons) all the time. Keep these in baskets or caddies in the center of tables.

- **Put supplies that are needed less often near centers.** Organize supplies that children will use less regularly in the writing, math, and other areas or centers discussed earlier. Keep these supplies in easy-to-reach, well-organized baskets or bins labeled with pictures and words.

- **Have a private storage area.** You'll need your own storage, not accessible to children, for extra supplies, plus special supplies such as paint, science materials, and social studies artifacts that may be messy, hard to replace, or appropriate only for occasional use.

- **Slowly introduce supplies.** To help ensure that children learn how to use and care for supplies properly, wait to put out certain supplies until you've formally introduced them. Begin with empty shelves and slowly add supplies as you teach and model their use. (See "Teaching Children How to Access and Maintain Supplies" on page 27.)

- **Rotate supplies.** Once you've filled the shelves, keep kindergartners engaged in their learning by occasionally removing some items and replacing them with others. Rotating supplies keeps shelves from being overcrowded and may lead to better care of supplies since you and the children will have less to manage.

More Tips for Supplies

- **Scrap box.** Have a box or basket in which children can place large unused scraps of paper. Not only does this teach children the importance of not wasting paper, it also provides them with interesting shapes for making collages or other projects.

- **Pencil sharpener.** While kindergartners have many talents, using the pencil sharpener wisely may not be one of them! Instead, teach children to place pencils that need sharpening in a basket. Sharpen the pencils when you have time, ask a parent volunteer to do so, or teach children how to do this as a classroom job.

- **Book return box.** Kindergartners, many of whom may not read well, can have difficulty putting books back where they belong. Early in the year, have a basket where they can place books when they finish with them. Reshelve books when you get a chance, or ask a volunteer to help. As the year progresses (and if children develop more organization skills), model and practice how to put books back in their proper places.

25

The Classroom Library

A well-stocked classroom library can foster a love of books in kindergartners. Children need books they can read and those they can't (but can browse and survey). Further, you'll want a wide variety of read-aloud books. Here are some categories to get you started (for specific title suggestions, see the appendix on pages 137–141):

- Emergent or beginning readers at many different levels

- Picture books from simple to complex

- Poetry and nursery rhyme collections

- Simple comic books

- Nonfiction books about animals, the way things work, world cultures, and so on

- Alphabet books

- Number books

- Pop-up books

- Board books (some kindergartners will still enjoy these)

- Class-created books

- Big books

Some ideas for stocking up fast:

- Use book clubs (such as Scholastic or Trumpet)—check for specials and how to earn bonus points for free books.

- Scavenge from other teachers—they often have extra copies.

- Visit garage sales or school book drives.

- Ask for parent donations.

- Check local library sales.

Sources of books for emergent readers:

- Rigby PM Books (http://rigby.hmhco .com/en/rigbyPM_ home.htm)

- Sunshine Books (www.award interactive.com)

- Learn to Read books published by Creative Teaching Press (www.creative teaching.com)

- Readinga-z.com (www.reading a-z.com)

Teaching Children How to Access and Maintain Supplies

Kindergartners are starting from scratch. They need you to teach and model in detail how to use, maintain, and store supplies. Break down supply routines into distinct components—and teach children each one. For example:

Interactive Modeling

See Chapter 2, "Schedules and Routines," pages 43–51, for a full explanation of interactive modeling.

■ **How to use supplies creatively.** Because kindergartners often see only one way to do things, give them opportunities to stretch their thinking about the potential uses of supplies. I try to guide them, within a structured context and clear expectations, in exploring many creative uses of materials. My strategy for structuring these purposeful explorations is to use the *Responsive Classroom* method of Guided Discovery (see box below).

■ **How to care for supplies.** Use interactive modeling to teach children the basics of taking care of supplies, such as how to make sure marker caps are on, how much pressure to use as they write with pencils or crayons, how to wind down glue sticks and put the tops back on, and how to put math materials back safely and quietly. Take photographs of children doing these things correctly and post them near supply areas for reference.

27

Learn about Guided Discovery at www.responsiveclassroom.org

One way to help children gain expertise with classroom materials is to use the process called Guided Discovery. This process focuses on observation, brainstorming, and exploratory play.

Guided Discovery is explained in more detail in *Learning Through Academic Choice* by Paula Denton, EdD (Northeast Foundation for Children, 2005) and in "Guided Discovery in Action" by Lynn Bechtel and Paula Denton (*Responsive Classroom Newsletter*, August 2004).

■ **How to find supplies.** Even if you've chosen the most effective organizational system ever, be sure to explicitly teach children about it. If you've divided your room into areas, slowly introduce each one to the children. If you're using pictorial labels for supplies and shelves, show these to them, too.

■ **How to put supplies back.** Teach kindergartners how to play a matching game when putting supplies back—for example, they match the label on a basket to the label on the shelf where the basket stays when not in use. (This kind of label or sticker system can also work well for teaching children how to shelve books.) Model for children how to check around their work area for missing parts or pieces. For some supplies, such as staplers and tape dispensers, post an outline of the shape on the shelf so that children can match the item to the outline.

■ **When to use supplies.** Kindergartners need some guidance about which supplies to use and when. Left on their own, they may find everything on the shelves interesting. Be explicit in your mini-lessons and directions—or place "Open" and "Closed" signs on shelves to guide their choices.

What if There Are Problems with Supplies?

Many kindergartners are explicit rule followers, so if they discover a broken crayon, a dried out marker, or a container placed in the wrong spot, they will most likely run straight to you. To avert unwanted interruptions, give children guidance here, too.

Have a box for problem supplies, and model for children what to do if they find something out of place (simply put it back in the right place!). Be clear, however, that they should tell you about big problems like paint spills.

Making Supplies Last

Kindergartners can quickly use up everything that you give them. Make the supplies go further by putting out only what children need for a short period of time. For instance, put out the amount of paper that you think children will need for two weeks. Put out enough markers to last for a month. Let children know if you have additional supplies and when you'll bring them out.

Although you will be focused on many things during the first weeks of kindergarten, pay some attention to the care children are taking with supplies. Do occasional "spot checks" to make sure children are caring for materials correctly and have put supplies back in the right place. And when they have done so, reinforce their efforts by letting them know that you noticed!

Classroom Displays

When I began teaching, I often covered the walls without thinking about what displays the children truly needed. It was more like decorating than teaching. These guidelines will help you avoid making the same mistake.

Some Guiding Principles

■ **Less is more.** Kindergartners will pay more attention to displays if you have fewer of them, but they're of high quality. Both walls and shelves should have plenty of open spaces so that the classroom feels calm and orderly. Remember to take down outdated displays or those that children aren't using. Avoid hanging things from the ceiling, which can be very distracting or even overwhelming to kindergartners.

■ **Make displays purposeful.** Make sure each display serves a definite purpose related to learning. If you put up children's work, is it to demonstrate their learning to classroom visitors? Or is it to show children the wide range of ideas they had on a project? Is a reference chart something you'll refer to often? Or is it something you just need once or twice? If you're not sure of a display's purpose, don't put it up. Thinking about displays in this way will help make the effort you put into creating them worthwhile.

■ **Share the display's purpose with children.** Let children know how a display can help them in their learning. For example: "I put up everyone's connections to the story we read. Over the next few days, try to notice all the different connections we had. Look at all the artistic ways we showed those."

■ **Use just a key word or two.** Many kindergartners are essentially nonreaders, so too much text can be overwhelming. Choose just a few essential words or phrases to post on displays—for instance, "Pets" could be the title for a display of children's drawings and writings about imaginary pets. Reference the words you display so that children will recognize them and their meaning.

Let Student Work Dominate

While there may be a few worthy commercial products to display (such as a calendar), children relate more to displays that they helped create. Start the year with mainly blank walls and shelf tops and slowly begin displaying children's work. Doing so tells them that the room belongs to them. (See Chapter 3, "Building Community," starting on page 65, to learn more about building community in the classroom.)

Here are some guidelines for displaying student work:

■ **Avoid "cookie-cutter" displays.** Kindergartners often think that there is only one way to do something, so putting up twenty-five variations of the same thing can reinforce this thinking. Help children broaden their perspective by making displays with diverse products. This way, as children try to learn new things, they can see how to reach a goal in different ways. For example, give children a few choices in an assignment, such as to solve a set of math problems by drawing pictures, working with manipulatives, or using pencil and paper. Then display their work or photos of it.

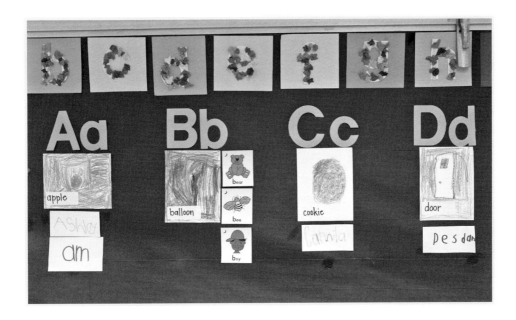

Or let children choose which of a few different assignments they want to display.

■ Include everyone. Because the range of abilities in kindergarten is wide, it can be tempting to display only the work of those who write clearly recognizable words or produce "clean" drawings. Resist this temptation. All children need to feel valued by having their work displayed.

■ Give children a say. Displays also have more value to children if they help decide what goes up to represent them. You could create a display area in your classroom with one square for each child. Add a small photo of each child along with his name to a corner of the square. Then let the children decide what gets displayed in the rest of their square and when to change things.

■ Include photos. Kindergartners pay close attention when they see photos of themselves or classmates posted. Take photographs of children being kind to one another, working at activities other

Put Displays at Eye Level

Whenever possible, put displays at the children's eye level. Kindergartners generally focus on objects close at hand. They may pay little attention to displays high up on a wall.

than pencil-and-paper tasks, playing cooperative games, or even sharing a peek at a new tooth.

■ **Plan for three-dimensional displays.** Kindergartners love to save their work with Legos and other hands-on materials. Use the tops of bookshelves or countertops to display such work. These displays also encourage children to notice different ideas and techniques for using materials. If you have limited shelf and countertop space, use photos instead. Help children make labels (and include their names) for their saved work.

Other Displays

■ **Yearlong charts.** You may want to have certain displays up all year long, such as class rules, a class calendar and birthday graph, and child-made alphabet and number charts. Avoid letting these become mere wall art, however. For example, refer to these displays often and teach children how to use them. If you find that no one is really using a chart, take it down.

■ **Current teaching tools or content.** You likely will need "anchor" charts for some lessons—for instance, a list of children's names can be used to display various letter sounds. Displaying anchor charts shortly after a lesson may be effective for learning as long as you demonstrate

Save Money—Avoid Commercially Made Charts

School supply stores and catalogs have thousands of charts for sale. However, not only are children more interested in displays that they made, but commercially made charts can get expensive.

If you want some anchor charts, such as an alphabet chart or a number poster, invite the children to help make them. Once I started doing this, I noticed the children paying a great deal more attention to these charts.

how to use them and then check that children are actually doing so. You can also group several anchor charts together on rings and hang them where children can review them.

Remember, it's easy to overdo anchor charts. Keep in mind that kindergartners primarily notice what is close to them and that they can get overwhelmed by visual clutter.

Technology

Kindergartners will most likely have a wide range of technology experience. Some may know more about computers than you do, while others may have little or no experience with using technology. However, even those with experience need to know the rules and expectations, such as which applications they can use and what to do when things go wrong.

Explicitly teach and model the use of all technology that children will encounter during kindergarten. Then give children time to practice what you show them so that they can become more independent and skillful in their use of technology.

Here are some guidelines for using technology, whether old (a tape player in the listening center) or new (computers and tablets):

■ **Focus on the basics.** Model and practice each step of how to use a computer, tablet, or other device. For example, demonstrate how to sit up straight at a computer station (children who learn poor ergonomic habits may develop health problems). Model how

Learn More about Classroom Setup at
www.responsiveclassroom.org

Classroom Spaces That Work by Marlynn K. Clayton (Northeast Foundation for Children, 2001).

33

to use the mouse and keyboard. Show children which buttons and keys they can press and which ones are off limits. Once they have the basic skills down, teach and model how to use a few developmentally appropriate applications.

■ **Use students as "tech helpers."** Despite the best teaching and modeling, some children may need more individual coaching when learning how to use technology. If you lack time for this, choose a child who is more comfortable with technology and invite her to help classmates.

■ **Share the technology.** Make sure all children, not just those who finish first or need an extra challenge, get to use these resources. Assign days or time slots, or invest in a software program that can randomly assign children to a device. Then post children's names when it's their turn to use the device.

■ **Supervise carefully.** Kindergartners need close monitoring, especially when they first use a resource. Try to station yourself close by so that you can monitor them. Or assign this task to a classroom aide or parent volunteer. Let children know what to do if they have a problem: Should they interrupt you, read in the book corner until you're free, or ask a designated adult or classmate for help?

■ **Set boundaries on Internet use.** Know your school's policies about children's Internet use, what blocks your school has in place, and what websites you're comfortable having children visit. Then teach children these boundaries.

34

Digital Cameras

You may want to have a digital camera both for your use and, if you're comfortable with it, for students' use, too. You can use the camera to create icons for displays (for instance, photos of students following the rules to go with each rule listed). Students may want to take photos on field trips or record other memorable moments in the classroom.

Yes, It's Cool. *But Do We Really Need It?*

New technology can be exciting, and we want children to be up-to-date. But if you have a say in what equipment goes into the classroom, exercise caution. Put technology in perspective with respect to everything else kindergartners need.

If you don't have enough books at an appropriate reading level, that might be a better place to start than a cool device that kindergartners use infrequently.

■ **Consider accessibility issues.** For instance, a child who uses a wheelchair might need certain accommodations when working at a computer station. Work with the experts in your school to ensure that every child can access the technology resources you plan to use.

Closing Thoughts

How you arrange and organize the classroom will have a powerful influence on how kindergartners learn and behave. A well-organized, uncluttered, and interesting classroom invites calm and focused learning. Children will thrive in a classroom where they have space to come together as a whole group; areas where they can work on their own; materials to spark their interest and imagination and meet their developmental needs; and displays that show their learning and progress. The time you put into setting up such a classroom, selecting supplies and other materials, and planning displays will help you and the children all year long.

CHAPTER 2

Schedules and Routines

After a few days of teaching kindergarten for the first time, I knew that I had to do something different with the schedule and in teaching routines, transitions, and behavior expectations. "Bite-size" became my mantra.

For example, I made the time I spent teaching in the circle area bite-size (no more than ten minutes or so). To teach children how to return to the circle area, I didn't model cleanups and transitions back to the circle all at once. Instead, I broke these routines into bite-size pieces. First, I taught what each detail of cleanup looked like and had the children practice each one. Then, I showed how to make a smooth transition back to the circle and had them practice that. Later, we put it all together. The difference this approach made to the children's success and the smooth running of the day was striking.

In this chapter, I help you take the bite-size concept I learned and apply it across the kindergarten day. You'll be able to set up your schedule and teach transitions and routines in a way that allows kindergartners to work and play together—cooperatively, actively, and productively.

Scheduling

Kindergartners need a school day that mainly consists of active, hands-on learning, interspersed with short and engaging instructional times. They also need some less-structured time, such as choice time and recess, to help them develop their imaginations, social skills, and verbal abilities. By following these basic ideas when making a schedule, you'll be supporting kindergartners in being productive and successful.

37

Consider How Kindergartners Learn Best

As you plan your schedule and lessons, consider these needs:

■ **Active, hands-on learning.** Kindergartners learn best by doing. Of course, you'll have to plan some direct instruction, but schedule most of their time for active learning. For example, during reading workshop, make sure that they spend most of their time engaging with the text in meaningful ways, such as reading texts at their level, highlighting words that meet a specific phonics pattern, or looking for words and images related to the five senses. At math, have them count, compare, measure, and weigh objects. During science, their hands should be on rocks, seeds, and other materials.

Even when you're doing direct teaching, find ways to make the learning more active. For instance, when teaching students how to sound out words, add physical movement to help them understand this concept. You could have students make a slight slicing motion (going from left to right) as they say each sound. Then, they slide their hand from left to right in one motion as they put the sounds together to form the word.

■ **Opportunities to interact and talk.** Kindergartners also need time to interact with peers. Some may still be "parallel talkers," and having many opportunities to interact with classmates will help them build skills to engage in two-way conversation. Many kindergartners also need to talk as they work. Developmentally, they literally must "think out loud" to think at all! While there should be some relatively quiet times, kindergarten should be lively for the most part.

■ **Encouragement toward independence.** Balance children's love of spending time with their teacher and their need to develop self-sufficiency. Try to schedule the day so that children have time to interact with you regularly, but also plan independent work times for them.

■ **Changes of pace and place.** Set up your day so that kindergartners have a varied pace to their activities, including movement within the classroom and outside. For instance, start lessons in the circle, move students to tables for independent work, and then have them return to the circle for reflection. Kindergartners also benefit from gross motor activities, so include movement in learning activities and use energizers throughout the day. (See Chapter 4, "Classroom Games, Special Projects, and Field Trips," pages 93–109, to learn more.)

■ **Less-structured times.** Although opportunities for self-directed learning and play are less common in schools today, kindergartners need these times. Playing (both outside and inside) provides key experiences from which children learn how to make good choices, get along with others, and talk about what they're doing in ways that structured academic tasks cannot provide.

■ Food and water. Kindergartners need to eat more often than just at a scheduled lunch time. Have periodic snack breaks or, if you have centers, work snack in as one of the rotations. Also, be sure children are well-hydrated— let them keep water bottles handy or use interactive modeling to teach them how to go to the water fountain independently.

Do You Need to Do Calendar Time?

Children may not fully solidify their learning about the passage of time until third grade. Moreover, children tend to grasp temporal concepts slowly and through experience, not through rote exercises. They may also become confused if extraneous elements, such as practicing the alphabet, are included in calendar time.

If you're required or want to do some calendar activities, consider these tips for making calendar time more purposeful:

■ **Have clear objectives** (for example, to learn names of months, days, and so on). Think about children's current understanding of calendar terms and temporal concepts when deciding on objectives. Tie calendar activities to those objectives, and assess whether children have met the objectives.

■ **Keep it simple.** Kindergartners tend to live in the "here and now." The basic calendar concepts they need to know are the month, the date, and the day.

■ **Tie calendar activities to real-life events.** For instance, use words and photos to highlight today's events and to mark past or upcoming events. Then discuss past and upcoming events in temporal terms such as "last week," "yesterday," and "in two weeks."

■ **Move noncalendar activities to other times of day.** Practice alphabet letters at reading time, math concepts at math time, and so on.

39

List the Day's Components

When making the schedule, consider the academic and social learning you want the class to do on most days. Here are the components I list when making a kindergarten schedule:

- Morning meeting
- Shared reading
- Read-alouds
- Reading workshop (might include literacy centers and small-group work)
- Writing workshop (full-day kindergarten might include interactive writing and minilessons; half-day kindergarten might alternate these)
- Choice time or centers (including explorations in content areas, art, and so on)
- Math
- Science
- Social studies
- Recess and lunch
- Quiet time (or rest time)
- Closing routines

Order the Day

What follows are some ideal schedules to use as the basis for creating full-day and half-day kindergarten schedules. Think about these schedule components and how much time you want to devote to each. While working with them, also consider components that you cannot control. Do you have an assigned lunch or recess time? Will your kindergartners be going to special area classes? If so, when?

Give Movement Breaks and Use Energizers Often!

Be sure to insert movement breaks and energizers throughout the day, not just when you can see that the children really need them. See Chapter 4, "Classroom Games, Special Projects, and Field Trips," pages 93–109, for more on using movement breaks and energizers.

40

Two Ideal Full-Day Schedules

Time	Activity	Time	Activity
7:45–8:00	Arrival routine	7:45–8:00	Arrival routine
8:00–8:20	Morning meeting	8:00–8:20	Morning meeting
8:20–8:40	Shared reading	8:20–9:10	Writing workshop
8:40–9:40	Reading workshop	9:10–9:30	Recess #1
9:40–9:50	Snack* (combine with quiet reading or a read-aloud)	9:30–10:30	Reading workshop
9:50–10:35	Math	10:30–11:00	Choice time or center time with snack included
10:35–10:50	Read-aloud, shared reading, or group singing	11:00–11:35	Science or social studies
10:50–11:20	Special	11:35–11:45	Read-aloud, shared reading, or group singing
11:20–11:35	Recess #1	11:45–12:15	Lunch
11:35–12:05	Lunch	12:15–12:30	Quiet time
12:05–12:20	Quiet time	12:30–1:20	Math
12:20–1:10	Writing workshop	1:20–1:40	Recess #2
1:10–1:45	Choice time or center time with snack included	1:40–1:50	Snack* (combine with quiet reading or a read-aloud)
1:45–2:20	Science and social studies	1:50–2:20	Special
2:20–2:40	Recess #2	2:20–2:40	Shared reading
2:40–2:50	Cleaning and packing up	2:40–2:50	Cleaning and packing up
2:50–3:00	Closing circle	2:50–3:00	Closing circle
3:00	Dismissal	3:00	Dismissal

*Snack consideration: In some kindergartens, it might work best to have a "snack station" that children can visit at designated times of the day. If you choose this option, you won't need a separate snack time. Make sure to carefully model use of this station.

Two Ideal Half-Day Schedules

7:45–8:00	Arrival routine
8:00–8:20	Morning meeting
8:20–8:30	Shared reading
8:30–9:30	Reading workshop
9:30–10:00	Choice time or centers with snack included
10:00–10:30	Math
10:30–10:50	Recess
10:50–11:20	Writing workshop
11:20–11:40	Science or social studies
11:40–11:50	Cleaning and packing up
11:50–12:00	Closing circle
12:00	Dismissal

7:45–8:00	Arrival routine
8:00–8:20	Morning meeting
8:20–8:50	Writing workshop
8:50–9:20	Math
9:20–9:50	Choice time or centers with snack included
9:50–10:50	Reading workshop
10:50–11:10	Recess
11:10–11:40	Science or social studies
11:40–11:50	Cleaning and packing up
11:50–12:00	Closing circle
12:00	Dismissal

Teaching Classroom Routines

When teaching routines to kindergartners, remember that school expectations are new to them. At home and in preschool, students may not have had to sit for extended periods, do assigned tasks, or share materials with  other children. Think about what expectations are appropriate for kindergartners. Once you have clarified these for yourself, teach students exactly what you expect. Then give them plenty of opportunities to practice and develop the necessary skills.

Use Interactive Modeling to Teach Routines and Behaviors

The best technique I have learned for teaching expected behaviors and routines is interactive modeling. It allows kindergartners to learn by seeing and hearing what *to* do, rather than what *not* to do. The table on page 44 shows what interactive modeling might look and sound like if you were teaching students how to stand in line safely and appropriately.

As discussed in Chapter 1, interactive modeling is also a powerful tool to show students how to use and care for materials. Page 45 shows how the technique might look and sound when you're modeling how to use scissors safely.

Do Students Know What Your Catchphrases Mean?

With the best of intentions, many younger-grade teachers use catchphrases to share expectations with students—for instance, "Criss-cross, applesauce" or "Inside voices."

No matter how clear these phrases are to us, they often have little meaning to students. So try to avoid these phrases. If you do use them, explicitly teach students what you expect. Or teach routines first and let students come up with their own phrases.

Interactive Modeling: Standing in Line

Steps to Follow	Might Sound/Look Like
1 Describe a positive behavior you will model.	"When we go outside to recess or go downstairs to music, we need to stay together. We're going to do that by walking in a line. Today, I will show you how to be safe in line. See what you notice."
2 Model the behavior.	Choose two students and whisper to them what you want them to do: Keep hands at side, plant feet, and look straight ahead. Position the two students in line about half an arm's length apart. (You may want to prepare the two students in advance or choose to do this modeling by yourself.) Remain quiet. You do not need to narrate as you model.
3 Ask students what they noticed.	"What did you notice about how we stood safely in line?" If necessary, follow up with questions—"How far apart were we?""What were our hands doing?""Where were we looking?" "What were our mouths doing?"—to prompt children to list the important elements: giving each person space, keeping hands to yourself, staying quiet, and looking ahead.
4 Ask a student volunteer to model the same behavior.	"Who can show us how to stand in line safely the same way Roberto, Anthony, and I did?"
5 Ask students what they noticed. (Repeat steps 4 and 5 with other student volunteers as needed.)	"What did you notice about the way Jon, Tre, and Sarah lined up safely?" The children name the three students' specific safe and appropriate line behaviors.
6 Have the class practice.	"Right now, I'm going to call a few of you up at a time to show us how to stand in line safely. I'll be watching and seeing you do all the things we just noticed."
7 Provide feedback.	"I saw everyone keeping about this much space between themselves and the next person [indicate keeping about half an arm's length apart]. I saw hands at your sides, mouths closed, and your eyes looking ahead of you."

Interactive Modeling: Using Scissors Safely

Steps to Follow	Might Sound/Look Like
1 Describe a positive behavior you will model.	"This year, we are going to use scissors to make many interesting things. But we need to use the scissors safely as we do that. Watch how I use scissors to cut out this shape in a safe and careful way."
2 Model the behavior.	Pick up the scissors and clearly demonstrate putting your thumb through the smaller hole and your other fingers through the larger hole. Hold the paper in your other hand and cut out a small shape from one corner of the paper. Put scissors down carefully when you finish cutting. Remain quiet. You do not need to narrate as you model.
3 Ask students what they noticed.	"What did you notice about how I used the scissors in a safe and careful way?" If necessary, follow up with prompting questions such as "Which fingers did I put in each hole?" "How did I hold the paper to make sure I didn't cut myself?" and "Where did I start the cutting? Why does this matter?"
4 Ask a student volunteer to model the same behavior.	"Who can show us how to use the scissors the same way I did?"
5 Ask students what they noticed. (Repeat steps 4 and 5 with other student volunteers as needed.)	"What did you notice about the way Lila used the scissors in a safe and careful way?" The children name Lila's specific safe and appropriate behaviors.
6 Have the class practice.	"Right now, you're all going to have a few minutes to practice cutting out shapes with scissors safely and carefully. I'll be watching and seeing you do all the things we just noticed."
7 Provide feedback.	"I saw everyone holding the scissors safely, with your thumb in the small hole and the rest of your fingers in the big hole. Everyone kept their other hand away and was very careful. It looks like we're ready to do some fun projects with scissors—safely and carefully!"

Keys to Successful Interactive Modeling

BE CLEAR ABOUT HOW YOU WANT THINGS DONE

Interactive modeling requires that you think through exactly what you want children to do. Knowing your own expectations for materials, routines, and behavior is essential. For example, exactly how do you want children to hold scissors? When teachers are inconsistent (for instance, letting students carry scissors sometimes by holding the blades and sometimes by grasping the handles), students become confused and behavior worsens. Take the time to think through each routine, talking to an experienced teacher if you need help. Also analyze a routine by thinking about what could go wrong.

More Benefits of Interactive Modeling

Students . . .

- Have more opportunities to participate (kindergartners learn best through this type of active and interactive learning)

- Become better observers (a skill that transfers into their academic work)

- Begin to value each other as models and sources of knowledge, which promotes community, trust, and teamwork

- Become better at monitoring their own behavior

USE A SCRIPT

Using a script for interactive modeling ensures that you actually teach what you planned to and speak concisely. The power of interactive modeling lies in demonstrating the behavior in a positive way and in students' being able to focus on its key elements. A script will help you stick to the few words necessary so students can focus.

PRACTICE BEFOREHAND IF NECESSARY

Sometimes an interactive modeling lesson, like the one on standing in line, requires that students help you demonstrate. Don't assume kindergartners will know what to do if you call on them in the moment to help demonstrate a behavior. Instead, find a time earlier in the day (or the day before) to practice with these students.

KEEP EXPECTATIONS HIGH

I was recently in a kindergarten class in which a teacher frequently had her students "turn and talk" about some aspect of her direct instruction. I was amazed at how on task these students were. It was clear that the teacher had modeled how this learning technique should look and sound and had given the students plenty of time to practice. However, she also kept a close eye on students as they talked to make sure that they stayed on topic. By holding the students to a high expectation, she ensured that their conversations were productive.

Your kindergartners will need time to practice and develop skills. Then, once they have a routine down, be vigilant—hold them to the high standard that they're capable of reaching.

ALSO KEEP EXPECTATIONS APPROPRIATE

Although you want students to meet expectations, it's equally important to keep expectations reasonable. Consider these common characteristics of kindergartners:

■ They often need to verbalize as they think and work. Expecting them to sit silently and work can be counterproductive.

■ Kindergartners often have difficulty sharing materials. They can do so, but don't go beyond their limits. For example, having only one blue marker at a table of four students is likely to invite trouble.

Consider what most kindergartners are capable of doing as you set up routines and schedules. This will help you set students up for success rather than for struggles.

Making Adjustments for Particular Students

Having high expectations is important, but so is recognizing an individual child's needs. Be prepared to modify expectations for certain students in certain circumstances.

For example, if you're modeling how to make eye contact when greeting another person, a child with autism may not be ready to do this. Modify the expectation as needed (for instance, by teaching the student to look toward the person or at her or his forehead).

Discuss with the class why you might modify rules at times. Explain that each of us needs different things to do our best and that it's the teacher's job to help figure out what each student needs.

GIVE STUDENTS PLENTY OF PRACTICE

Just like academic skills, behaviors and routines take practice and time for students to learn and perfect. Kindergartners need multiple opportunities to practice, and they need coaching and feedback. For example, after teaching them how to walk in line, continue setting aside time for them to practice. As the children practice, let them know how they're doing: "I see students keeping up with the person in front of them just like we practiced. I see everyone safely looking ahead!" Before going on to a new task or skill, reinforce what they're doing well—and reteach anything they're struggling with.

KEEP THE PRACTICE ENGAGING

Be careful not to make practice seem dull or punitive. You may not even want to call it practice. For instance, when practicing expected lunch behaviors, you could say, "On the way to school, I stopped and got some delicious fruit so that we could play lunch today. Who remembers what our goals are for lunch?"

Also, look for ways to make practice more engaging. When practicing how to move between centers, for example, challenge students to move without your hearing a peep. Or, when practicing how to come quietly to the circle, challenge students to pretend they are walking on a soft, springy bed. Once they get to the circle, have something interesting for them to do: "I put up a page from an *I Spy* book. When you get to your spot in the circle, quietly see how many things you can find that start with the letter *b*."

Remember the importance of breaking routines into "bite-size" chunks for kindergartners? Think about these examples:

- When teaching about glue sticks, do one lesson on how far to roll the stick up, a way to gently apply glue to the paper, and then how to roll the stick down. Do another lesson on other ways to apply glue to paper, incorporating skills learned in the first lesson, and ending with where to store the glue sticks. Do a third lesson to inspire thinking about creative things to make using glue sticks, paper, and scissors—after you've modeled safe use of scissors!

- When teaching expectations for writing workshop, teach one step at a time. First, teach what it looks like to pay attention during the instruction part of a writing mini-lesson. As a separate step, teach students how to partner chat during the mini-lesson. Then, teach what it looks like to return to one's seat and start on the writing part of the mini-lesson. Later, teach what to do with writing papers when time is up and how to clean up one's space. You'll also need to teach how to come back to the circle area for the reflection part of the lesson.

Think about what might go wrong and scaffold for those eventualities, too. Although many teachers have students bring their writing to the circle with them, picture twenty-five kindergartners, all holding pieces of paper. Do you really want students to have their papers at the circle? If so, have them put the papers behind their spots while they await instructions for what to do next.

49

When to Reteach Routines

Here are a few times when students will benefit from extra attention to routines:

- Monday morning

- Friday afternoon

- Right after vacation

- Before and after you've had a substitute teacher

- Around the holidays

- When a new student joins the class

- Before assemblies and field trips

REINFORCE SUCCESS OFTEN

Kindergartners thrive on your approval. They need to hear exactly what they're doing correctly—it lets them know that they're on the right track, reinforces what they're learning, and builds a positive learning community. Be sure to give them plenty of positive reinforcement when they accomplish routines, do tasks, and meet behavior expectations.

Name the specific behaviors that you saw students doing well: "At recess today, people shared swings, jump ropes, and sidewalk chalk. You really took good care of each other." "You were all talking to your partners about our topic of something we like to do at home. You are ready to write!" "Everyone lined up quickly after lunch. You are really working on making sure that no one has to wait for you."

When giving positive reinforcement, try to keep the "pleasing-the-teacher" aspect out of it. Maintain a focus on students' learning and on the classroom community's needs. For example, avoid saying, "I like the way everyone rolled the glue sticks down," which puts the focus on how you, the teacher, feel pleased about what the children did. Instead, try "Everyone rolled the glue sticks down the way we all practiced so they'll stay in good shape for us to use." This emphasizes the children's positive choices and use of well-learned skills.

Here's another example: Instead of saying, "Thank you for listening during our writing mini-lesson," which conveys that gaining your appreciation should be the children's most important goal, try "You were all listening carefully during our mini-lesson." Again, this kind of reinforcement tells children that they are in control of doing appropriate behavior.

GIVE INDIVIDUALS PRIVATE ATTENTION IF NEEDED

Some classes find certain routines particularly challenging, but even within those classes, some students will have mastered the routines. Be sure to let these students know in private that you see their success: "I noticed that you are always on time to the circle. You are always ready to learn!"

If a few students are struggling with routines after the rest of the class has them down, give them extra practice, modify expectations, or station yourself closer to them. For all students, pay attention to growth. Don't wait until students are perfect to reinforce their progress. For example, say to a student privately: "You used to have trouble stopping playing at recess. But this week you were on time three times. That's your best record yet!"

Key Routines to Teach

RESPONDING TO SIGNALS FOR ATTENTION

The first—and most important—routine kindergartners need to learn is when and how to pay attention to you. You cannot teach, give instructions, or keep kindergartners safe if they do not know how to stop, look, and listen when you give a signal for quiet and attention. Give students plenty of practice learning these signals.

The ideal signal is something calming and respectful, such as the sound of a gentle chime or the teacher silently holding up her hand. Yelling or talking over children's voices gives the message that it's okay for us to interrupt them and that what they're doing is not worthy of respect. It also can raise the energy level in the room, making students less likely to focus on what you're saying even if you do get their attention.

Whichever signal you use, make sure you have everyone's attention before speaking. Waiting too long, however, gives the impression that students do not need to respond quickly to your signals. If individual students have trouble with the signal, practice individually with them, move closer to them, or assign a "buddy" to help them.

Learn More about Positive Teacher Language
at www.responsiveclassroom.org

The Power of Our Words: Teacher Language That Helps Children Learn by Paula Denton, EdD (Northeast Foundation for Children, 2007).

In general, I use two kinds of signals: visual and auditory.

■ **Visual signal.** Visual signals—such as a raised hand—work best when students are close to you and each other. Use a visual signal, for instance, when they are seated in the circle area or when you are working with a small group. I raise one hand high and put the fingers of my other hand over my lips. Children who see this gesture stop what they're doing, become quiet, and copy the signal. Having something to do with both hands helps kindergartners gain control over their bodies; covering their lips is a helpful reminder to refrain from talking.

■ **Auditory signal.** The raised hand signal doesn't work as well when students are scattered about the room. At these times, an auditory signal such as a chime, a rain stick, or another instrument with a pleasing tone works well. Use interactive modeling to show the students what to do when they hear the sound: Stop what they're doing, put all materials down, stop talking, put a finger to their lips, place their other hand at their side, and look at you. An option some teachers use is to have students stand up and cross their arms to help them avoid the temptation to keep working with the materials.

Pitfalls When Using Signals

■ **Speaking before everyone is quiet.** Sends the message that not everyone has to respond to the signal.

■ **Inconsistency in using signals.** If you say you're going to use a signal but then fail to do so consistently, children may become confused: Is the signal important or not? Do you really mean what you say and say what you mean?

■ **Repeating or using more than one signal.** Teaches students that they don't have to comply right away—they can wait for the second (or third) signal.

■ **Demanding immediate silence.** Students have a natural need to get to a stopping point in their conversation or work (ten to fifteen seconds should do it).

■ **Saying "I'll wait until . . ."** Telling students "I'll just wait until everyone is ready" gives them the message that they don't have to respond in a timely way and can take as long as they like.

■ **Modeling the "wrong way."** Creates a competing mental picture that will confuse students.

Having a Substitute Teacher? Keep the Schedule and Key Routines in Place!

Schedules. It may be tempting to plan something different to make the day with the substitute, or "guest teacher," feel more special. But kindergartners may feel anxious or even upset by having a substitute, so they'll feel more comfortable if the usual schedule and routines are maintained.

Routines. Be specific in your lesson plans about any special routines or traditions the class has. For instance, if you typically play a book on tape during snack time or sing a song during cleanup, make sure your plans reflect that.

Other ways to help the day go smoothly:

■ Choose several students whom the guest teacher can ask about the schedule and routines (rotate among students during the year).

■ Discuss with students ways they can care for each other and the guest teacher while you're out (do what the guest teacher says even if it's different from what you would do, remember that you'll be back tomorrow, and so on). Leave these ideas for the guest teacher to review with the class.

■ Use interactive modeling to teach and practice being with a guest teacher. For example, have a colleague pretend to be the guest teacher and act out doing letter activities in the wrong order. Model and practice how to do the activities in that order or how to respectfully let the guest teacher know the correct order.

Remember to make practicing the signal fun. For example, practice some of the skills for responding to the signal by playing a "freeze" game at morning meeting. Children can dance while music is playing, but must immediately freeze when it stops. Make a direct connection between their success with this game and responding to the signal: "I saw everyone freezing when the music stopped. Today, when I ring the chime, let's see if we can do the same thing."

STUDENT SIGNALS

Kindergartners will also need some signals to get your attention. Think about the various situations throughout the day when they might need to do so. Then teach them simple, nonverbal signals that will not disrupt whole-group work or your work with individuals or small groups.

■ **Taking a turn to speak in a whole group.** When students need your attention in a whole-group situation, they could raise their hand or make a question mark signal.

■ **"I need to go to the bathroom."** It is important to let kindergartners go to the bathroom when the need strikes. Teach them a signal for letting you know that they need to go and show them what your response will look like. Children could raise and shake a fist, and you could nod your head in recognition. Teach children that it's okay to come to you if you're not seeing their signal. Practice with them how to come to you quietly.

- **SOS for emergencies.** Teach students a separate signal to use if they or someone near them has an emergency. Define what an emergency is—a bloody nose, feeling sick, a bathroom accident, and so forth—as this is not a natural concept for kindergartners. An SOS signal—hand shut, hand open, hand shut—works well. Be sure to tell students that it is always okay for them to come directly over to you during an emergency, rather than use a signal. Teach and model how to come quickly and calmly over to you during these times.

BATHROOM ROUTINES

In addition to the signal for when to go, kindergartners need to know these aspects of the bathroom routine: how to tell if the bathroom is occupied, how to signal that they're in the bathroom, how much toilet paper to use (and where it goes after it's used), being sure to flush, washing hands afterward, wiping around the sink, and quickly returning to whatever the class is doing. Kindergartners need to start learning this routine on the first day of school. Because they may be especially excited or nervous on that first day, many will need to go early and often!

Take all the children into one bathroom to model and practice expected behaviors. Do frequent checks on the bathrooms during the first few days of school to make sure your expectations for cleanliness are being met. Be sure to give positive reinforcement to students for returning quickly and getting right back to the task at hand.

Make a system that students can use to indicate who is in the bathroom so you won't have to keep track mentally. You could use a pocket chart that contains cards with every student's name and a separate pocket chart with boys' and girls' slots for the bathroom cards to go in. When they need to go to the bathroom, students move their cards to the slot and return their cards to the pocket when they come back. Or, upon receiving your okay signal, students could take a designated bathroom pass and place it by you. They would return the pass to its storage spot when they come back.

Even with the best systems, teaching, and practice, kindergartners sometimes have bathroom accidents. Store extra pairs of clean underwear and multipurpose pants (sweat or knit pants work well) in a variety of sizes, or have each child keep an extra set of clothes at school, depending on school policy. Accidents happen for different reasons—but if a child has multiple incidents, contact the family to discuss what might be going on.

Never shame a child for accidents and encourage families not to do so either. Even for "frequent fliers," let children go as needed. If children sense that they might not get to go when needed, it can exacerbate a problem.

Also, take the time to teach, model, and practice what to do if someone has an accident. Begin by asking students to think about whether they have ever had an accident and how that felt. Ask them to brainstorm how they can take care of classmates if an accident happens (go get a teacher, use kind words, keep working, and so on). Model and practice what a few suggestions would look and sound like. Be ready to take the whole class to the bathroom after this discussion, as it will prompt a need to go!

MORNING ROUTINES

Once kindergartners get used to school, some may still experience shyness or anxiety upon arrival while others may arrive bursting at the seams with excitement. For all of them, having a calm and consistent morning routine will help them be at their best. Some things to consider in planning the morning routine:

■ Check-in. Many kindergartners need frequent teacher time, so give them some right off the bat. If your students arrive on a staggered schedule, allow time for greeting each child individually and spending a few minutes finding out what is happening in their lives. If your students arrive all at once, greet them as a whole group, but then circulate for quick, private conversations.

How to Teach Line and Hallway Routines

Decide where the line should be. Choose a spot with few distractions where all the students can stand comfortably in line before they leave the classroom.

Teach exactly how to line up. For kindergartners, this may involve several different modeling lessons:

■ What order to line up in (devise a table-by-table or other system, and teach it)

■ How to stand in line (see page 44 for a detailed interactive modeling example)

■ How to walk in line (keep pace with the person in front of you, stop when that person stops, eyes ahead, hands at sides)

Teach expected hallway behavior. It can be hard for kindergartners to pay attention to the person in front of them and have a conversation at the same time. As a result, have children be quiet at the beginning of the year when learning the line routine. Once they've mastered the basics, consider adding quiet talking to the line routine. If

you do, model and practice exactly what volume is okay. Otherwise, you may spend too much time turning the volume down.

Walk with your class. Kindergartners aren't ready to walk as a class without their teacher; they also wouldn't feel safe doing so.

Teach how to stop. Model and have students practice stopping at predetermined places. Give feedback, reminders, or redirections as needed.

56

You may learn that someone had a particularly rough morning and needs to sit next to you. Or you may see that a typically active child has even more energy than usual. You might send that child on a quick errand with a teaching assistant or give him frequent movement breaks throughout the day.

■ Individual activities. To help students enjoy a smooth start to the day and have time for a quick check-in with you, provide a few quiet activities for them to choose from upon arrival. Avoid tasks that will require too much preparation or cleanup. Some activities that work well include browsing through books, using math manipulatives, and drawing.

■ Putting away backpacks, coats, and other materials. Kindergartners need to learn how to put away things from home safely and efficiently. They also need to learn what to do with toys and other items brought from home (for example, these must remain in backpacks or be placed in the special share spot).

- **Sign-in.** To avoid having to spend time taking attendance, many teachers have students mark their presence in some way. They might answer a question on your morning message, practice writing their names by signing an attendance book, or  move their name card from one pocket of a chart to another. If a lunch count is needed for the cafeteria, teach and model how children can note their lunch choice on their own as part of the morning sign-in routine.

- **Notes from home or turning things in.** Be sure to have a designated routine for how students hand in notes from home and any work they had to do.

SITTING IN THE CIRCLE FOR WHOLE-GROUP LESSONS

Sitting and paying attention during a whole-group lesson does not come naturally to kindergartners. Be sure to explicitly teach them what it looks and sounds like to pay attention while in a whole-group circle (and why this matters). Show them how to sit up straight, providing back support for any student with weak trunk control. Also, be clear about what to do with their legs and how to direct their eyes and bodies toward the person speaking.

As the year goes on, you may want to teach other accepted ways to show listening, such as nodding at a speaker or demonstrating a connection to what someone is saying with a thumbs-up. When you practice sitting up and paying attention with the class, begin with small steps and short periods of time. Slowly expand these, based on the children's progress and your learning goals for them. And remember, keep your instructions specific and brief.

TRANSITIONS

Like herding kittens . . . that's what came to mind when I first tried transitions with kindergartners. But these transitions can go more smoothly—if you think them through and break them down into manageable parts. Teach and model each part. Give students time to practice and reinforce their successes.

Remember to Teach Recess and Lunch Routines!

See Chapter 3, "Building Community," starting on page 65, to learn about these middle-of-the-day routines.

57

Kindergartners especially need time to prepare to change gears. Give them a "heads-up" signal a few minutes before time is up. Then they can use their remaining time to finish what they're doing and get ready to transition to the next activity. This "heads-up" lets children know that you value their work and helps them practice positive work habits.

Transitions within the classroom:

■ **Moving from the circle to independent work spots.** Kindergartners are not yet masters of efficiency, so teach them exactly how it looks to leave the circle and get right to work at a table or center. Organize lessons so that you can send small groups of children off at the same time. Sending students one by one takes too long; sending everyone off at once can lead to confusion. As small groups get to work, take a moment to watch the transition. Reinforce the successful behaviors you notice: "I see so many children already starting their projects. People are safely getting what they need and planning how to work carefully."

■ **Moving back to the circle.** Kindergartners need guidance here, too. The goal is for children to bring their work to a close peacefully, with enough time for cleanup and a smooth transition back to the circle. Think about each step of this process and teach each one carefully: what to do when they hear the heads-up signal, how to clean up, where to put materials, what to do with their work, how long cleaning should be, and what path they should take to the circle. For cleanups of messy tasks, put small trash cans atop each table instead of having everyone use one large trash can. Also, kindergartners may better understand how long a transition should be if you play a short piece of calming music. When the music ends, all students should be finished with cleanup.

Have a System in Place—for who goes first and who gets to handle prized responsibilities. For example:

■ **A job chart.** Assign each student a job for the day or week. Jobs might include line leader, door holder, plant waterer, and so forth. You could make a pocket chart with one pocket for each job. Move students' name cards from one job to the next as needed.

■ **Drawing names.** Draw names out of a bag to see who does a particular job at a given time.

■ **Groupings.** Call students to line up by table groups or other categories.

Transitions into and out of the classroom:

■ **Bring classroom work to a peaceful close.** Transitions out of the classroom work best if students are given a heads-up signal and have time to bring their work to a natural, unhurried close. If possible, have students clean up and come to the circle for a quick reflection before leaving the room. Even if you don't have time for such a closing, make sure students can finish, clean up, and become quiet wherever they are.

■ **Play lining-up music.** Kindergartners generally love music, so you may want to have a short piece playing as the "line-up song." Choose something that is fun yet calming. Once the children are in line, give them a few seconds to pause and take a deep breath before you signal them to begin walking.

■ **Give line tasks.** Giving students something to do or think about as they walk in line helps them stay calm. ("On our way to music, look for things you see that have a triangle shape. When we get there, whisper in my ear one thing you saw.")

59

■ **Have consistent routines for returning to the classroom.** Transitions into the room go smoother if students follow the same routine each time. For example, have the line leader stop at the door. While students pause, make sure everyone is calm before entering the room. Give reinforcement if possible: "Ms. Baker said that you listened to directions in music, played beautiful songs, and took good care of each other!" Then, have students gather in the circle area upon entering the room. Direct them to focus their attention on something once they get there: "I've put four shapes up on the chart stand. Take a look at them. Then, look around you to see if anything in our room has one of those shapes."

■ **Be a careful observer.** Kindergartners feel safest when they sense that we are paying close attention to them. As the class walks to and from the room, and as they return to the circle area, give them your undivided attention. Be ready to reinforce or redirect students as needed.

Many kindergartners have a tendency to get up, roam around the room, or seek out their teacher for praise or help during independent work times. Anticipate these tendencies. Use interactive modeling to teach students how to stick with an assignment and what to do if they encounter difficulties. Some key points:

■ **Staying in one place.** Model and practice what it looks like to get materials quickly and stay in one spot to complete a task. As you begin practicing independent work, start with relatively short work periods (five to ten minutes) so that students feel successful meeting this challenge. (Kindergartners can work on one task for longer periods of time, but build up to this gradually.) Explain that this skill matters because it helps them complete their own work and helps classmates to concentrate on theirs.

■ **Talking and noise level.** Because many kindergartners need to verbalize and interact with others as they work, demanding complete silence may impede their productivity. Of course, if the talking is too loud, students will have trouble focusing on the task. Model and practice what an acceptable noise level sounds like. Try playing quiet background music. Tell students that if they cannot hear the music, they are too loud. Then redirect them just when they start to get noisy—students are more likely to stay on track if you intervene early.

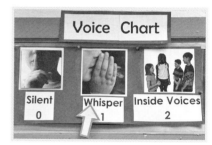

■ **What to do if they're "stuck."** Model and practice ways for children to get help without interrupting you. For instance, teach them how to seek help from classmates and how to give help when asked. Also, have alternate assignments ready for kindergartners to work on if friends cannot help (for example, read from a book bin, do an activity with spelling words, or write in a journal). Let students know when you'll be coming around to see if anyone needs help.

■ **Scaffolding independent work practice.** After you've modeled independent work time, let students practice with you close at hand. For example, once most students seem to have the independent work routine down, do some work with a small group who may still be struggling with this skill. Give this group fairly easy work to accomplish so that you can give most of your attention to observing and giving feedback to the "independent" workers.

Done well, read-aloud time can be the best time of day for kindergartners! Even those without much prior exposure to books can quickly become entranced by them. I find that kindergartners especially love the Mo Willems *Pigeon* series (they very forcefully tell the pigeon "no"

when he asks to do forbidden tasks). They relish books that are silly, such as Robert Munsch's *We Share Everything*, and series books featuring the same characters, such as Lauren Child's *Charlie and Lola* books. Listening silently to these types of books can be very challenging for kindergartners, so allow for active participation, giving them guidelines for how this might look and sound.

- **Model and practice responses to read-alouds.** Choose a book that calls out for participation (for example, Mo Willems' *Don't Let the Pigeon Drive the Bus!*). Each time you read, model how loud the "no" and "okay" should be and what to do with your body while saying these words. Continue to reinforce the message that students do not have to be perfectly silent but should participate in positive ways.

- **Tell students what kind of book you're about to read.** If a book has some repeating lines that students can say with you, questions to which they can call out answers, or surprises that they can react to, tell them this ahead of time. Similarly, when you're reading a book that calls for quiet listening, such as Philip C. Stead's *A Sick Day for Amos McGee*, prepare students for that as well.

- **Schedule effectively.** Kindergartners benefit greatly from several well-timed read-alouds each day. Schedule these for times when they've sat back down after moving around a bit. Keep your book introductions short so students can focus on the reading.

> **Learn More about Schedules and Routines**
> at www.responsiveclassroom.org
>
> *The First Six Weeks of School* by Paula Denton and Roxann Kriete (Northeast Foundation for Children, 2000).

- **Scaffold for success.** Set students up for success with read-alouds by beginning the year with easier-to-read books that call for more active participation. Gradually increase book length and complexity. When moving to

61

longer books, consider a series with the same set of characters (such as *Frog and Toad*, *Little Bear*, or *Poppleton*). Being familiar with the characters helps kindergartners deal with the longer text. Keep this in mind when moving to even longer chapter books.

EMERGENCY ROUTINES

Students should know how to take care of themselves and each other during classroom emergencies. Teach children what to do when "disasters" like the following occur: someone has a temper tantrum, gets a bloody nose, or throws up. Signal verbally ("This is an emergency time") or nonverbally (use your auditory signal and show the SOS sign), and make sure students take these steps:

■ **Students keep working.** If they're working independently, just keep working.

■ **Students read at their seats.** If they're meeting in the circle, they get a book, return to their table spots, and start reading.

Making sure students have mastered this routine will give you the space to take care of the occasional emergency quickly and efficiently.

DISMISSAL ROUTINES

Kindergartners need to learn a calm dismissal routine so that they can leave the classroom safely and happily. Because kindergartners are often tired at the end of the day, have as few dismissal tasks as possible. For example, have students clean tables as part of their table work routines. Then, when it's time to leave for the day, students will only need to pack backpacks, get coats, and line up for dismissal.

As with all essential classroom routines, teach dismissal during the first week of school if possible. Do this early in the day when kindergartners have more energy. At the end of the first week of school, set aside a little time to fine-tune, modeling dismissal procedures again if children seem to need it. In addition to the nitty-gritty parts of dismissal, leave time for a quick closing circle. Sing a fun song together, do a quiet energizer, or reflect on the day's positive events ("What kind thing did you do today?" or "How did we follow our rules?").

OTHER ROUTINES

Some other routines and social skills you may want to model and practice:

- How to share materials

- Completing class jobs

- Closing circle

- How to rotate among centers or activities

- Caring for and putting away supplies

- Winning and losing a game graciously

- Fire, earthquake, or tornado drill routines

- Greeting friends and family at school

- Indoor recess routines

Learn More about Closing Circles at www.responsiveclassroom.org

"Closing Circles: A Simple, Joyful Way to End the Day," *Responsive Classroom Newsletter*, February 2011.

Closing Thoughts

Taking the time to carefully plan a kindergarten schedule and to teach the routines required to make it work may seem daunting. But the efforts you put into planning the day and teaching even the most seemingly basic tasks will pay rewards throughout the school year. Students will be able to devote most of their time to the great social and academic learning that kindergarten has to offer. Just as importantly, you in turn will be able to devote most of your time to observing students and teaching them these skills.

CHAPTER 3

Building Community

Kindergartners who feel secure at school and have a sense of belonging within their classrooms do better in school. They're more willing to take the risks necessary for learning, they're more motivated, and they don't have to meet their social needs in negative ways. Taking the time to build a strong sense of community will be essential, both for your students and for you.

I remember what a difference community made during one of my more strenuous kindergarten teaching days. It was midyear, and a new student who had just joined our class was crying. As I comforted him, another student had an accident at her seat. Then a student from the class next door came to tell me that their substitute had not arrived. I quickly assigned a few classmates to help John, the new student. They ushered him to the book corner and started pulling out their favorites. I sent the girl who had the accident to change into the extra clothes we had stored in our classroom; then I asked two of her friends to sit beside her chair and keep others away from it. I gathered my colleague's class into their room and had each student read with a classmate while I waited for the guest teacher to arrive, observing both classes from the doorway we shared. This class also had a very strong sense of community; everyone did exactly what was needed.

Within twenty minutes, the substitute had arrived, I had cleaned up the accident, and my class had launched into a happy, welcoming morning meeting. Before the meeting, several students suggested greetings and activities to help John feel better. For the rest of the day, John happily took part in every activity.

Building a strong community will help your kindergartners (and you!) throughout the school day, especially an unusually rough one like the one I've just described. In this chapter, I offer some guidance on forming strong bonds, with emphasis on helping students get to know each other, planning successful celebrations, and ensuring that recess and lunch are the productive, social times that they are meant to be.

Teacher Tone and Demeanor

Through your kind and respectful treatment of all students, you can provide a strong model for children to emulate. Kindergartners can be very single-minded, seeing only one way to do things. Many also care a great deal about what their teachers say and do. As a result, most will follow your lead when it comes to how to treat others. If you are friendly and kind to everyone, children will try to do the same. If you have a positive, nonjudgmental tone (even when someone misbehaves), they will be more understanding and forgiving of others, too. If you model empathy when someone is having a bad day, students will do so as well. Your tone and demeanor will go a long way toward creating a classroom community that feels safe and welcoming.

When Speaking to Kindergartners . . .

Talk to kindergartners using the same tone and cadence you would use with adults. Talking in a sing-song cadence or high-pitched tone can give the impression that we see kindergartners as pets or as incompetent people. Also, avoid talking about students or letting others discuss students in their presence as if they were not there.

■ Treat everyone with respect. Respect has many facets—our facial expressions, tone, body language, and the words we choose. Take a nonjudgmental stance and use respectful words and an even tone with all students, even when redirecting or giving consequences for inappropriate behavior. Kindergartners imitate us. If they see us making a harsh face, using a ridiculing tone, or becoming impatient, they likely will do so also.

■ Get to know each child. Take the time to get to know each student. Spend some private time with each one every day, if possible. When we know what a child is interested in, what upsets or worries her, or what his life is like outside of school, we can care for and teach that child better. When our students see us spending time with each classmate, it sends a powerful message: Every child matters.

■ **Demonstrate empathy and compassion.** Kindergartners can be quite self-centered; they need help seeing things from another point of view. You can demonstrate empathy and compassion for others in many ways. When a child makes a mistake, respond calmly and nonjudgmentally. Keep the focus on helping students solve problems and move ahead. If a student is having a rough day, demonstrate caring in your words and actions.

■ **Model positive feedback.** When your kindergartners see you giving them positive and specific feedback, they more likely will be positive with each other. I was always excited when I overheard students use "I notice" to point out something a classmate had done well. A student might say, "I noticed that you included a lot of details in your picture." Kindergartners thrive in a classroom where compliments are given frequently.

■ **Speak about the class as a whole.** One powerful way to build community is to address your class as one group: "Today, our class will get to learn a new game at recess. I want to hear what you think of it." Mention the qualities of community (caring, teamwork, cooperation) that you're seeing the class as a whole demonstrate: "During reading workshop, I saw students helping each other sound out words. I saw other students help their friends figure out what to do when they were stuck. Everyone kept the volume at a 'just right' level. You are taking good care of each other so we can all learn."

Greetings

The line from that old *Cheers* TV show theme song—"Sometimes you want to go where everybody knows your name"—could not apply more to kindergartners. They feel important and connected to their classroom community when their names are known and when they are welcomed in a warm and friendly way every day.

Of course, one of the first greetings will come from you. Try to have your day planned and materials ready so that you can greet children by name as they enter the classroom. Sit on a low chair so that you'll be at the children's eye level.

Begin the day with a structured way for students to greet one another, such as part of the morning meeting. This will set a positive tone for learning and help the children feel safe and significant within the group.

Students have to learn the skills of greeting, but they need to do so gradually and in a variety of formats. At the simplest level, children could pass a friendly "Hello, _____ [classmate's name]" around the circle. Teach them to use a kind face, make eye contact, and speak in a friendly voice loud enough for everyone to hear. On other days, use a more playful approach with singing or chanting that involves naming every classmate. (See "Good Greetings in Kindergarten" on page 70 for more ideas.)

Make the most of greeting times, but also give students chances to learn names and feel welcomed at other times of day. Here are some tips:

■ **Model greeting skills.** When taught appropriately, kindergartners are capable of friendly, warm, and even sophisticated greetings. As with all kindergarten skills, begin with the basics. Use interactive modeling (see page 69 for an example) to show exactly what a warm and friendly greeting between two people looks and sounds like. Also, model what other students should be doing when two students greet each other—turn their bodies and eyes toward the greeters and honor the greeting with quiet attentiveness.

CONTINUED ON PAGE 72

Interactive Modeling of Greetings

Steps to Follow	Might Sound and Look Like
1 Describe a positive behavior you will model.	"Today, I'm going to greet each of you in a friendly way. Then you'll have a chance to practice greeting me in the same friendly way. Watch and see what I do as I greet Mira."
2 Model the behavior.	"Good morning, Mira." Use a friendly tone, show a friendly face, and turn your body so you're facing the student.
3 Ask students what they noticed.	"What did you see me do when I greeted Mira in a friendly way?" (If necessary, follow up with questions— "What kind of voice did I use?" or "What did you notice about my body?"—to prompt children to list the important elements: friendly voice, friendly face, body turned to the person, used her name, and so on.)
4 Ask student volunteers to model the same behavior.	"Now Mira is going to greet me back in the same way. Watch and see what she does."
5 Ask students what they noticed. (Repeat steps 4 and 5 with other student volunteers as needed.)	"What did you see Mira do to greet me in a friendly way?"
6 Have the class practice.	"Now we're all going to practice. I'm going to come around the circle and greet each of you. I'll be watching and seeing you do all the things we just talked about."
7 Provide feedback.	"As I went around the circle, most of you smiled at me, had friendly eyes, and called me by name. Tomorrow, we'll greet each other again."

Good Greetings in Kindergarten

Beginning of Year

Focus on the basics of greeting (turn body toward the person, show friendly face, use greeting words and the person's name).

- **Teacher greetings.** Greet students individually around the circle, modeling correct name pronunciation, appropriate voice and facial expressions, and so on.

- **Around-the-circle simple greetings.** Pass a friendly "good morning" or "hello" around the circle with no handshake or other body contact.

- **Greeting assigned partners.** Turn photos of students face down in the middle of the circle. Students quickly choose one and greet the person pictured. Or have students draw cards from a deck. Children with matching cards (same letter of alphabet, same number) come to the middle and greet each other.

- **Chant greetings.** Kindergartners respond especially well to these. Here's one greeting kindergartners enjoy: "_____ is here. _____ is here. It's a great day because _____ is here."

To acknowledge the importance of every class member, even those who are absent, add at the end, "_____ isn't here. _____ isn't here. We're a little sad because _____ isn't here."

Continue until all class members have been named.

Middle to End of Year

Vary greetings so that students still practice the basics but also try more complex greetings.

- **Physical greetings.** Shake hands, give high fives, or bump fists. Use interactive modeling to teach how to do these physical greetings safely and in a friendly way.

- **Foreign language greetings.** Kindergartners enjoy learning how people in other countries say "hello." (Rachel Isadora's book *Say Hello!* can be a great way to introduce greetings in various languages.)

- **More playful greetings.** Look for ways to add fun to greetings. For example, let students roll a ball or toss a beanbag to the person being greeted.

- **More complex chants.** Add chants that require movements or more complex interactions. For instance, students could turn to their neighbor and chant and move to "Hello, neighbor, what d'ya say? It's gonna be a wonderful day. So, clap your hands and boogie on down. Give a little bump [students gently bump hips] and turn around."

- **Song greetings.** Many music artists such as Dr. Jean have greeting songs that work well to start the day.

Ideas for Learning Names

Kindergartners benefit from fun and engaging practice in learning each others' names. Just be sure that whatever idea you use honors the name that students prefer (first name? nickname?) and its proper pronunciation (seek parental help if unsure).

■ **Display of students' names.** As soon as possible, build a display with everyone's name and, if available, a photo. Build into the first few days of school games and activities that will help children learn each other's names.

■ **Simple name games and songs.** Sing "Where is _____?" to the tune of "Frère Jacques." ("Where is _____, where is _____, there s/he is, there s/he is, we're so glad you're here, we're so glad you're here, yes we are, yes we are.") Play "Who Stole the Cookie From the Cookie Jar?" or give clues about a student and see how quickly students can identify her. Or create concentration bingo games using names and photos. Play the games as whole-group or center activities.

■ **Personalized name tags.** Have students decorate name tags to wear and place on their desks and cubbies so that their names are visible in several places. Have students wear name tags for the first few days of school and when you have a substitute teacher.

■ **Class books.** Make class books with a page devoted to each child. You could use children's books such as Bill Martin Jr.'s *Brown Bear, Brown Bear* and make a new version, replacing animals' names and photographs with those of children. Or make a mini-book for every child with each page featuring one simple sentence and a photograph of that child. Once children have created books about themselves, place the books in the classroom library so students can read them at independent reading times.

■ **Other academic activities.** Put children's names in a pocket chart and help them sort according to which names have the same number of letters or which start or end with the same letter.

CONTINUED FROM PAGE 68

■ **Scaffold for success.** Once students have the basics down, such as a warm and friendly face, eye contact, and using the other person's name, begin adding new skills. For instance, you may want to teach students to use a gesture such as a handshake. Or have students add customary greeting words such as "How are you?" As always, model and practice each of these skills as you add them.

■ **Focus on learning names throughout the day.** Engage students in a variety of other activities that require them to use or read names. (See "Ideas for Learning Names" on page 71.)

■ **Do chants often.** Kindergartners can also learn names and practice greeting skills through the repetition of rhymes, songs, and chants. Hearing names frequently in chants such as "_____, _____, s/he's our friend, let's give a cheer and do it all again! Hooray!" teaches name recognition and builds a sense of community.

■ **Have children say good-bye.** Children can also practice names and the same skills used in greetings by occasionally saying good-bye to each other in a closing circle at the end of the day.

72

Getting to Know Each Other

To deepen the sense of community in your classroom, give children frequent opportunities to share information about themselves with each other. This sharing can take many formats, but whatever format you use, be sure that the sharing is engaging and meaningful. Avoid or modify the traditional "show and tell" structure, which often results in students' sharing what they have, not who they are. Also, take the time to teach students how to speak clearly and succinctly to avoid the mumbled, rambling discourses that sometimes lead kindergarten listeners to tune out.

Structures for Sharing

STRUCTURES FOR EARLY IN THE YEAR

■ **Around-the-circle, one-word sharing.** Model the basics of sharing at the simplest level—speaking clearly and at a loud-enough volume, and demonstrating appropriate listening—by having each student simply share one word on a given topic during morning meeting. Choose an accessible topic for kindergartners such as a fruit they like to eat or favorite color. Use interactive modeling to teach how to share a response and what the job of listeners is. Then, in an around-the-circle format, let each child have a turn to share. Follow up with a quick listening game: "Who remembers who liked blue (red, and so on)?" Knowing they'll be playing "Who remembers" encourages children to listen carefully during the sharing.

■ **Around-the-circle sharing using sentence frames.** Once students have the basics of sharing down, try sentence frames built around interesting topics. Some possible sentence frames:

- ❖ My favorite animal is _____ (could also be a game, sport, book, movie, and so on).
- ❖ One thing I like to do at home is _____.
- ❖ After school I like to _____.
- ❖ I think I am good at _____.
- ❖ One thing my family and I like to do is _____.
- ❖ One thing I did this weekend was _____.
- ❖ My favorite thing about school so far is _____.
- ❖ My favorite place to be is _____.
- ❖ Something I like to imagine is _____.

Use interactive modeling to show how to use sentence frames. Continue to follow up with listening games from time to time: "Stand up if you can tell us someone who shared that she likes to play basketball."

■ **Object shares.** Kindergartners can also get to know their classmates better by sharing certain items from home. Be sure the items tell something about the student—a family photo, a book they like to read with their families, or something they made. Teach students how to briefly describe what they brought and why: "I brought a photo of my family. You can see my mom, my stepdad, and my two stepsisters."

■ **Class books.** Students can learn about each other by creating class books together. For instance, you could read Nancy Carlson's *I Like Me!* and then have students create their own pages, listing and illustrating what they like about themselves.

■ **Parts of a whole.** Create displays in which students draw, write, or share something about themselves. If you have a bulletin board with space for each student, invite students to display a family photo, a drawing of a favorite book, and so on. Coordinating these displays with the sentence frame shares or the object shares can also extend children's interest in learning about each other. For another display, have each child create a quilt square for a class quilt or a puzzle piece that forms a whole when joined with other pieces.

STRUCTURES FOR LATER IN THE YEAR

74

■ **More detailed sharing.** As the year progresses, teach children to share in more detail about a given topic. To ensure that each child has the time to do so and that others listen, have only one to three children share per day and assign topics. With the whole class, brainstorm a list of topics that students think their classmates want to share about themselves. The list might include games they like to play, things that they do with their families, or funny moments. Teach kindergartners the skills of extended sharing—staying on topic, being brief, and, as always, speaking at an appropriate volume. Here are some tips:

❖ Use interactive modeling to show what it sounds like to say one main point and give details about it. For example, I might say when modeling, "My dog Mudge is always getting in trouble. Once he ate a whole can of peanuts. Another time, he chased a cat into our basement. The poor cat didn't want to come out." Make sure students notice that you stayed on topic and how many sentences you shared.

❖ Make the concepts of staying on topic and being brief concrete by using objects such as Unifix cubes: Students say one sentence for each cube.

❖ Use sentence frames: "This weekend I went to _____. I went with _____. We had a _____ time because _____."

■ **Writing assignments.** Let students create simple books about themselves. A book might have the following pattern:

❖ Hi, my name is _____.

❖ I like to _____.

❖ I don't like to _____.

❖ I like to eat _____.

❖ I don't like to eat _____.

> **Learn More about Sharing at**
> www.responsiveclassroom.org
>
> *The Morning Meeting Book*
> by Roxann Kriete (Northeast
> Foundation for Children, 2002).

Students can make the pages over a series of days and illustrate each page. Since it's hard for kindergartners to project as they read or to keep an engaging pace, let students "share" their books by having you read their text while they stand next to you. Keep the books (or copies) in the classroom library so students can read them again and again.

STRUCTURES FOR THE WHOLE YEAR

■ **Pop up.** Students are all seated. They "pop up" when you say something that is true about them: "Pop up if you have a brother." "Pop up if you like strawberry ice cream with whipped cream on top." Students can stay popped up until everyone is up or sit back down for each round. Model appropriate popping up.

■ **Would you rather?** Offer students a choice and let them go to a designated area in the room to represent their answer. Choices could be realistic—"Would you rather play outside or play inside?"—or fanciful—"Would you rather jump into a giant bowl of jelly or a giant bowl of potato chips?" Of course, model how to walk safely to an area.

■ **"If You're Happy and You Know It."** Adapt this song to be a sharing song by singing it like this: "If you really like _____ (basketball, swinging, etc.), clap your hands, if you really like _____ clap your hands, if you really like _____ and you really want to show it, if you really like _____, clap your hands." Students who agree with the "like" statement clap their hands, stomp their feet, and so on.

See Chapter 4, "Classroom Games, Special Projects, and Field Trips," pages 93–109, for more information on these and other classroom games and activities.

Keeping Sharing Safe for Everyone

Students often need our help recognizing what news is appropriate for sharing and what should be kept private or shared only with a teacher. Ideas for giving this help:

- Brainstorm appropriate topics with students. Post the list.

- Give examples of private and public information. Private: "My brother had a big argument with my mom about homework." Public: "My brother and I made up a new game together."

- Have students check with you first if they're unsure. Tell students if they're ever unsure whether something should be shared, they should check with you first.

- Check in with the day's scheduled sharers. If a topic is inappropriate, help the child find another topic.

- Enlist parents' help. Explain the goals of sharing. Let parents know that if the family has any unsettling news, they should talk with their child about sharing it only with you.

- React calmly if a student does share something inappropriate. This sometimes happens despite our best efforts. Stop the sharing calmly, try not to embarrass the student, and move on. For instance, "Anna, that sounds like something you and I should discuss privately. You and I will talk, and then you can share about it or something else tomorrow."

Class Celebrations

Celebrations help kindergartners feel closer to each other, become more excited about learning, and realize that what they are doing at school is valuable. However, celebrations can overwhelm or overstimulate students—and tax parents or you—if they're too involved or require too much preparation. Yet celebrations don't have to be elaborate to feel special to students. Indeed, when celebrations are fun and simple, they keep the focus on what is being commemorated, not on having a party for a party's sake.

What to Celebrate

To come up with celebration ideas, first think about the purposes for kindergarten celebrations. In general, they should help students learn more (or become interested in learning more) about a topic. They might also show families and the school community what content the class has been learning or what skills children have mastered. Celebrations can also give kindergartners a chance to collaborate with their families or other classes to see how the skills they're learning connect to life outside of school or to later school experiences. Of course, celebrations can also be a great way for the class to recognize and acknowledge the learning they've done, simply for themselves.

If you identify the reasons for a celebration, you'll have an easier time planning what to celebrate and how, and the event will be more relevant to students' learning. The celebration will also be more likely to generate the excitement about learning, the community-building, and the school-home connections you're seeking.

Ideas for Kindergarten Celebrations

Area	Possible Celebrations
Language arts	**Publishing party.** Students share their published pieces with families, other classes, or selected teachers and staff.
	Author birthday. Get a calendar of children's authors. Celebrate an author's birthday by reading a book or series of books and exploring what makes that author's work special.
	Poetry party. After children have learned several poems and developed accompanying movements, invite guests to watch a performance. Follow up by having guests read a poem with students.
	Theme, genre, or author party. For instance, to mark the end of a unit on Eric Carle, students and their guests could make a page for a big book based on his artistic ideas and techniques. The celebration would end with a sharing of the pages. Afterward, bind the pages together and keep the book in the classroom library.
Math	**___ day of school celebrations.** Although students traditionally celebrate the 100th day of school, you could also celebrate other landmark days—10th day, 25th day, and so on—with activities to mark each number.
	Game day or hour. Children play games with guests or older students to practice math skills in fun and meaningful ways.
	End-of-unit party. At the end of a unit on measuring, students could have a measuring scavenger hunt or a measuring Olympics.
Social studies and science	**Science day or hour.** For instance, have a "science festival" during which students rotate through a series of science centers or investigations.
	Museum day. Convert your classroom to a temporary museum with exhibits related to a particular science or social studies topic.
	End-of-unit party. At the end of a unit on their town or city, invite members of the community (police, local hospital workers, and so on) to visit, share, and see what the students have achieved.

Ideas for Kindergarten Celebrations

Area	Possible Celebrations
Social curriculum	**Friendship celebration.** Celebrate the children's accomplishments in learning how to be kind and caring friends. Play friendship games and do activities related to friendship. Highlight specific acts of being a good friend that you've noticed.
	Student birthdays, "student of the week," or "family of the week." For birthday-related events, sing a variety of birthday songs throughout the day when children need a movement break. For "student of the week," invite someone from the child's family to visit and share one of the child's favorite books. For "family of the week," invite members of the family in for a "family interview" and to share a special snack. Display family photos and lead an activity based on their interests.

Tips for Successful Celebrations

■ Clearly communicate the purpose to students and parent helpers. Keep the focus on the "why" of the celebration (whether it's to showcase skills students are currently learning or have already mastered or to generate excitement about an upcoming unit). This focus will help everyone involved with the event: Students will learn more, guests will be clearer about their role, and classroom volunteers will be better prepared.

■ Help students have appropriate expectations. Explain to students what they will be doing at the celebration. That way, they won't be disappointed by an event not living up to their imaginative expectations. Explaining what they will be doing also helps students understand and meet behavior expectations for the event.

■ Keep it simple. Remember, kindergartners often appreciate more understated celebrations. For example, a publishing celebration could begin with everyone in a large circle. Next, students could share a class poem or class book they wrote. Then, students could sit at a "station" with their own published pieces. Guests would rotate among students and leave each a compliment, using note cards or stickie notes. To close, students and guests could share a round of singing or a snack.

■ **Use parent volunteers wisely.** If a celebration requires parents or other adult helpers, use the guidelines in Chapter 5, "Communicating with Parents" (pages 111–135), to assign appropriate jobs. Also, if family guests are involved, make sure that each child will have a guest. (Invite administrators or special area teachers to be guests of students whose families cannot make it.) Families can also participate in an "absentee" way. For instance, a family that could not attend a math game party could donate a snack. Or, if they have a favorite math game, the child could bring it to school to share during the party. Let the class know how the families who are not present have participated in the celebration.

What about Holidays?

Celebrating academic events and achievements generally provides more valuable learning experiences and positive reinforcement for students than commemorating traditional holidays. Because kindergartners tend to be fairly excitable and hold high expectations for holidays, a more traditional holiday party can result in struggles with behavior and loss of focus on learning. In addition, choosing holidays that are common to all families is a big challenge. There are plenty of kindergarten milestones to celebrate that don't run the risk of causing any child or family to feel uncomfortable or left out.

However, if you are required to have certain holiday celebrations, here are some ideas to make them more inclusive and successful:

■ Halloween. Kindergartners love to dress up, so invite them to come to school dressed as favorite book characters. Or you could help them make and wear "guess-the-letter" costumes. If you've just finished a friendship unit, have them come as one of the friends of a famous friendship pair. Don't overburden families with costume-making. Instead, help children make costumes in class and enlist school colleagues or older students to help. At the party, have snacks and activities related to the theme you chose.

■ Winter holidays. Let students share a story, game, tradition, food, or artifact from a winter holiday their family celebrates (include New Year's Day as a choice for students who do not celebrate religious or traditional cultural holidays). Another option is a winter-theme exploration during which you read books about winter, study winter weather in different parts of the world, learn about animal hibernation, and so on. End the unit with a winter festival.

■ **Valentine's Day.** As a holiday of love, Valentine's Day is the perfect time to encourage students to focus on others. They could plan and throw a party for the school's office, custodial, and cafeteria staffs. They could study letter-writing during the weeks leading up to Valentine's Day and then write letters to a military unit stationed overseas, to senior citizens at a local nursing home, or to children at a local hospital.

Recess

Kindergartners are active and energetic, and their gross motor skills are rapidly developing. They need recess time to run and play. This time also provides opportunities for them to interact with classmates as they explore common interests, learn how to play group games, or sing a jump rope song together. Plus, those kindergartners who need a little extra adult attention can often get it at recess.

Recess, however, will not automatically lead to these desired results. Kindergartners need teaching and guidance to make the most of recess. How do they safely use all the playground equipment? What happens if someone gets hurt? How do they invite someone to play with them or ask to join a game?

If kindergartners aren't explicitly taught the rules and expectations for recess, many will experience stress during this time. They may feel left out ("I wanted to play that game, but they didn't ask me!"), hurt ("Sally told me I couldn't go to her birthday party if I played with Kendra!"), or unsafe ("I'm not playing that game if I don't know the rules!").

Kindergartners can feel safer and be more successful at recess when we take the time to carefully introduce and teach the skills required—and when we supervise and monitor their behavior closely. We also need to give positive reinforcement to students when we see them doing the behaviors we've taught and practiced.

Advocate for Different Types of Play

To make recess happier and more meaningful for all students, talk to your school leaders about offering several different play options if current choices seem limited. Some children may prefer organized tag and large group games. Others may want to swing, slide, and climb on playground structures. Many enjoy playing in the sandbox, jumping rope, playing hopscotch, drawing with sidewalk chalk, and blowing bubbles. Kindergartners also enjoy playing imagination-based games at recess and benefit from having an area for these games.

> **Recess Rules!**
>
> Remember to teach and model any specific recess rules your school has. If your school doesn't have specific recess rules, teach children how to apply their classroom or schoolwide rules to recess—show them what those rules might sound and look like in different playground situations.

Teach Recess Behaviors

During the first few weeks of school, devote some class and scheduled recess time to teach all the skills kindergartners need for success at recess. Begin by teaching and modeling a few specific skills that children need to have to make their first recesses safe and fun. Start these lessons in the classroom and then go outside so children can see these skills modeled on the playground and practice them there.

For example, teach and model how to avoid collisions by watching out for others and by keeping a safe distance from them (about an arm's length) as you move about. Also, teach and model:

- The recess "freeze" signal

- Staying within play area boundaries

- Responding to the lining-up signal

- Coming back into the building

In guiding children's practice, make a game out of "playing" the basic skills you just taught. You could define the boundaries for an area that's big enough for the class to move around in. Then "play" staying in the boundaries while walking without colliding, responding to the "freeze" signal, lining up, and so on. Focus these first sessions on showing children how to play safely, with kindness and friendliness, just as they would do in the classroom.

Remember that children need to learn the basic rules and skills, but they also need to have some free and active play. So try to keep things fun and relaxed. After a few days—once children have demonstrated they know the basic skills and rules—teach and play a quick whole-class game, such as a simple tag game.

Also, be sure to teach and model these other recess skills and behaviors during the first days of school:

■ Getting an adult's attention

■ Helping someone who's hurt

■ Circling up to hear further instructions about a game

■ Getting permission to go to the bathroom

Keeping Tag Games Safe for Everyone

Model and give students time to practice several key skills to make sure tag games are safe for all:

■ **Where and how to tag.** A basic rule is to tag only on the back between the shoulders and hips. A tag should feel firm but gentle.

■ **Avoiding collisions.** Reinforce your earlier modeling about how to watch out for others and keep a safe distance as children run and try to avoid getting tagged.

■ **Tagger's choice.** Make sure students understand that if the person tagging believes he or she has tagged someone else, that person has to freeze even if she or he disagrees.

Stop games at the first sign that students are getting rough and repractice these key skills. If just one student has trouble with any of these skills, have that student take a break from the game. At a later point, review and practice the expectations with the student.

Introduce Recess Choices

After using whole-group games to teach initial recess skills, slowly introduce other recess choices. Teach, model, and explore each recess choice and its ground rules. Then let students practice each choice for a day or more. This way, students will fully understand the rules and expectations for each recess choice.

Teach, model, and let children practice how to:

- Make a recess choice

- Use particular structures (swings, slides, etc.)

- Get and put away equipment

- Share equipment

- Ask someone to play with them

- Join a game already in progress

- Resolve a problem they're having with someone (see "Dealing with Conflicts" on page 85)

Observe and Support

Recess will be much smoother with careful teaching, but still stay in touch with what is happening at recess and do additional teaching as necessary. If you don't have recess duty, talk to the monitors and your students. Occasionally visit recess to see how students are doing. As you gather information, provide positive feedback to the class about what's going well.

Be alert for individual students who may need further support. Look out for:

- Children playing alone. Some children enjoy playing alone, but usually children are not doing so by choice, so be ready to intervene. With the child's permission, assign a series of recess buddies and check to see how things are going. Or spend a few days running group games and include the child. Teach all children to be on the lookout for those who need a friend or playmate.

■ Exclusionary play. Kindergartners sometimes devise games that exclude certain people ("It's a fairy princess game. He's a boy!"), or they exclude others out of anger (many kindergartners say "you can't be my friend" or "you can't come to my birthday party" when they're mad). When teaching recess behaviors, discuss how recess games and play are meant to include everyone so that everyone can get exercise and have fun. Then, if exclusionary play does occur, you can use this concept as a reference point when intervening to help children learn how to be inclusive and express anger in an appropriate way.

■ Rough play. Some kindergartners like to play in a very physical way. Others may not have developed spatial awareness and may crash into other students while running, making this kind of play feel too rough for some. Give students, especially those who tend toward overly physical play, more guidance about what appropriate play at school looks like.

Dealing with Conflicts

Here are some tips to help prevent conflicts during recess and to help students resolve them if they do occur:

■ Be proactive. Teach students the difference between issues that are worth doing something about and those that are not. Sort through various scenarios as "little" or "big" issues (for example, a child saying a jump rope rhyme wrong vs. one child hitting another child).

■ Skip the "no tattling" rule. Students need to know that when they have a problem, adults can help. You may want to do some teaching and coaching about which issues to report and which ones to live with, but having a blanket "no tattling" policy allows problems to fester and some students to dominate others.

Learn More about Handling Tattling at
www.responsiveclassroom.org

"What to Do about Tattling" by Margaret Berry Wilson, *Responsive Classroom Newsletter*, April 2011.

■ Teach conflict resolution. Most kindergartners need adult guidance to use basic conflict resolution structures, so be sure to use kindergarten-appropriate techniques. See Chapter 3 in *Solving Thorny Behavior Problems: How Teachers and Students Can Work Together* by Caltha Crowe (Northeast Foundation for Children, 2009); book available at www.responsiveclassroom.org.

Learn More about Indoor Games and Recess at www.responsiveclassroom.org

36 Games Kids Love to Play by Adrian Harrison (Northeast Foundation for Children, 2002).

"Rules Talk: Promoting Positive Behavior Every Day," *Responsive Classroom Newsletter*, February 2011.

Other Resources

Elementary Teacher's Handbook of Indoor and Outdoor Games by Art Kamiya (Parker, 1985).

The Ultimate Playground & Recess Game Book by Guy Bailey (Educators Press, 2000).

Play with Students

If you have recess duty, make the most of it by taking an active role in children's play. Walking around the playground, playing tag games with them, and pushing them on swings helps you to interact with students and see them in different contexts. Even if you don't have recess duty, go outside and join in occasionally—students will be thrilled and you'll learn more about them.

Check In with Students

Even if you can't go outside for recess, check in with students afterward to see how recess went. You can do this privately as students enter the classroom: "When you get to the room, whisper to me whether your recess was fun or not so fun." Or wait until everyone is settled in the room and ask for a thumbs-up/thumbs-down signal. You can also have class meetings in which you ask some open-ended questions: "What has made recess fun for you so far?" "What do you need more help with at recess?" "What do you think you could do to make recess more fun for everyone?"

Lunchtime

Eating in the cafeteria can be both daunting and exciting for kindergartners. Like recess, lunchtime offers children the opportunity to meet their physical needs and their social-emotional needs for connecting and interacting with classmates. But without adult help, lunchtime can also feel unsafe or unsettling. Kindergartners will greatly benefit from your help in navigating lunch. By making it a time when children have the space and freedom to eat, talk, and laugh with classmates, you'll help ensure that they return to the classroom refreshed and ready to learn.

Teach Lunchtime Behaviors

The bite-size approach (no pun intended!) works especially well for kindergarten lunch. If you break down the lunch process to figure out every routine that students need to know to make lunch successful, you may find that lunch is quite complex for children. So consider having students eat lunch in the classroom for the first few days of school. (Check whether students have to bring lunches in from the cafeteria or if the cafeteria staff will deliver lunch.)

During these first few days of school, use interactive modeling to teach some lunch basics:

■ Staying in your seat

■ Using table manners (for example, keep food on tray, chew with mouth closed)

■ Safely opening milk or juice containers, utensil packets, and so on

■ Signaling a need to use the bathroom

■ Throwing away trash

■ Handling spills and cleaning tables and floors

After teaching these basics in the classroom, take the class to the cafeteria at a noneating time and begin teaching the other parts of lunch that they need to know:

■ Lining up for food

- Handling the tray, plate, utensils, drinks, and so on

- Making selections quickly and sticking to the choices you make

- Using polite manners with cafeteria staff

- Paying or using a ticket system

- Responding to the signal for attention

- Lining up for dismissal

- Remembering to eat with all that's going on in the cafeteria!

Assign Seats or Tables

To make sure that all kindergartners have someone to sit with at lunch and a chance to get to know a variety of classmates, assign lunch seats. Here are some easy ways to assign seats or tables: Make table groups for the week (and place "name tents" on the tables), assign lunch buddies, or have students sit with the same people they're currently sitting with in the classroom.

Teach and Model Conversation Skills

Kindergartners are still learning what a real conversation looks and sounds like, so lunch is an ideal time to practice these skills. The children will benefit from your devoting some classroom time to various conversation skills. Some tips:

- **Teach appropriate lunchtime topics.** Provide kindergartners with ideas for topics that are suitable for lunch and those that are not (such as parties to which not everyone is invited, the time they threw up on the dentist, or how loud their dad can burp). It often helps to build on what you discussed during sharing

Interactive Modeling

See Chapter 2, "Schedules and Routines," pages 43–51, for a full explanation of interactive modeling.

times. A sample list of appropriate topics might look like this:

- ❖ Siblings
- ❖ Family events or pets
- ❖ Sports
- ❖ Activities outside of school
- ❖ TV shows, movies, or books
- ❖ Games you play at recess
- ❖ Favorite foods

■ **Model turn-taking in conversation.** Once you have a list, choose a few topics and use interactive modeling to demonstrate the give-and-take of a conversation. If you can, use another adult or older student for this interactive modeling. If that's not possible, ask a student to help out, but practice with him before modeling for the class.

■ **Practice and give positive feedback.** Pair students up, provide a topic, and have them practice the conversation skills of balancing talking and listening, making kind remarks, using friendly faces, and staying on topic. Give positive feedback for these important behaviors.

■ **Check in occasionally.** Follow up on your teaching by checking in with students. During lunch, spend a few minutes going from table to table to specifically notice the positives in their conversations. Even if you don't have lunch duty, drop in to the lunchroom from time to time to see how students are doing. This is especially useful to do early in the school year and after vacations so that you can reinforce positive behaviors.

■ **Regularly assign lunchtime conversation partners and topics.** You can spark excitement in having rich lunchtime conversations by challenging students to find out as much as they can about their lunch partner or about a topic that the whole table discusses. Upon their return from lunch, ask students to report what they learned. List what they say on the board or chart paper to help increase their excitement about learning and strengthen their sense of community.

Eat with Students

Eating lunch with students from time to time will benefit both you and them. You'll be able to see what your students are doing well and reinforce those things. You'll also see what skills they need to have retaught and what new skills they're ready to learn. Students will also be thrilled to have a few extra minutes to talk with you—and in these conversations, you can get to know them even better.

Plan a Calm and Quiet Ending to Lunch

Kindergarten lunch can be noisy and feel too energized. Help students make the transition back to the classroom by taking the energy level down during the last few minutes of lunch. You can use interactive modeling to teach this routine:

■ An adult gives the signal for attention and lets students know that they have five minutes left.

■ During these last five minutes of lunch, students focus on finishing eating and getting ready to return to the classroom.

■ Students also bring the noise level down. Model what this sounds like (students often find it quite entertaining to practice going from high to low).

■ At an adult's signal, designated tables begin discarding their trash and either returning to their seats or lining up.

Closing Thoughts

Kindergartners thrive when they're part of a strong, caring community of learners. Being part of a community helps children feel excited about and confident in putting forth their best effort on every task. You help build this community when you carefully model what kindness and respect look like; plan thoughtful and energizing greetings, sharings, and classroom celebrations; and deliberately take steps to help recess and lunch go well. You also help build community when you take the time to get to know your students and for them to know each other. Doing so helps every child feel significant and safe at school. This work of building community takes time, but it is time very well spent.

CHAPTER 4

Classroom Games, Special Projects, and Field Trips

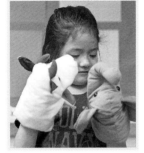

Play is a gateway to learning and building community for all children. And kindergartners love to play! Playing games with classmates can reinforce their academic skills and content learning. Games also enable kindergartners to learn self-control and other social skills in a fun way. Plus, playing, smiling, and laughing together help the children feel more connected to you and their classmates.

In the same way, kindergartners thrive when school includes special projects and field trips. Like games, these events give children a chance to learn, practice, and apply academic content or skills in new and exciting ways. They also provide children with rich social experiences that help fulfill their need to feel part of a group.

One year, our kindergarten class took a trip to the Los Angeles Zoo. That event stood out as a highlight of the year. The children loved having a whole day outdoors, spending time together, and studying the animals. I had never seen them so happy and engaged. And, when we returned to school the next day and reflected on our learning, their engagement continued. With great attention to detail, many wrote about animals that they had discovered and drew pictures of what they had seen. I overheard "arguments" between students over small details of the animals: "Its beak was yellow!" "No, it was more orangey-red!" When we sat together to write a group thank-you note, the students clearly wanted to make sure the "zoo people" understood how special the trip was for them.

You'll want to make sure your kindergartners have rich outside experiences, special projects within the classroom, and daily experiences of fun and community by carefully choosing games, songs, and other activities. In this chapter, I give you ideas for what is feasible for kindergartners and how to make these special learning times productive.

Classroom Games and Songs

There is something quite inspiring about children singing a beloved song together or laughing as they play a silly game. They bring a particular earnestness to these activities—the joy and sense of community they experience from singing and playing are very evident. But singing, chanting, rhyming, and playing can also take a class off track if you do not choose wisely, model these activities, and monitor students' energy level.

Because repetition is so important for kindergartners' learning, make sure there's plenty of repetition in their games, songs, and chants. Remember, though, to balance repetition with variety so that you help children gain confidence and learn how to stretch themselves to meet a new challenge. For example, teach a simple song. Once the children know the tune and lyrics, vary the words or add movements. Here are some more tips for making games and songs successful:

Finding Time for Lively Learning

Teachers, even kindergarten teachers, often feel pressure to cut out games, activities, field trips, and special projects because they worry that these may detract from academics. Hard as it may be, try to resist this pressure.

There is no reason for lively learning to compete with academics. Make games, activities, events, and projects purposeful and tie them to the curriculum. For instance, you can help children develop phonemic awareness through clapping, listening, and singing games. Children can learn counting or even spelling through song.

It *is* possible to have fun while focusing on academics!

Foster Cooperation

Games should help students move and release energy—and learn valuable social and academic skills. Games should also be joyful. All too often, competitive and elimination games work directly against these goals. Competitive games are usually joyful only for the winners, and competition can easily teach the wrong kinds of social skills. Also, during elimination games, most children are forced "out" and have nothing to do for much of the game. Their lack of engagement can lead to problems.

Instead of competitive or elimination games, choose games that allow all students to be fully engaged and to work together. Here are a few of my favorites to play with kindergartners:

■ **Cooperative Musical Chairs.** This variation on traditional musical chairs is best played after children have experience with the "freeze game" (see Chapter 2, "Schedules and Routines," page 53). Place chairs in the circle. While music is playing, children move and dance around the circle. When the music stops, they find a chair and sit in it safely. As you slowly begin to remove chairs, students must work together to make sure everyone can still sit safely. When teaching this game, model sitting safely. Then invite ideas about how students can share chairs and sit safely once chairs are removed. Model key behaviors needed to carry out their (reasonable) ideas.

95

■ **What Did I Do?** This game can be played in many ways. At its simplest, classmates study the person who is "it." Next, they close their eyes while that person changes one thing about her appearance. Then students try to guess what has changed. Be clear that the person who is "it" needs to change something visible. Vary this game by having students notice something you change in the classroom, a word you change in a pocket chart, a number you add to a number line, and so forth. Another variation can help students develop phonemic awareness: Say three sounds (/b/ /a/ /t/). Then, repeat them, but change one sound (/m/ /a/ /t/). Keep the pace of the games moving so all students keep thinking and stay engaged.

■ **This Is the Way We _____.** Begin with the traditional song, "Here We Go Round the Mulberry Bush." In stages, teach students how to sing the song, move as a group around the circle, and make motions to accompany the lyrics. Then begin adding your own lyrics and movements (students can help with this). For instance, kindergartners could sing, "This is the way we tiptoe around, tiptoe around, tiptoe around," as they hold hands and tiptoe around the circle. Add in academic learning with lines like these: "This is the way we move to the left [right, forward, and so on]." "This is the way we count back from ten." "This is the way we rhyme words with _____."

Scaffold

Kindergartners have relatively short attention spans, even for fun games and activities. For a game, chant, or song that has many variations, start with the simplest version. For instance, in teaching the chant, "Tony Chestnut" (find the words and tune online), first teach the melody and lyrics. During another session, teach the accompanying movements. Later, add other variations, such as moving quickly to the song or doing it in slow motion.

Build in Cooldowns

Energizers, chants, and games help students burn off excess energy and refocus their attention. However, some may get students too energized and, without our help, they won't be able to rein in their silliness or enthusiasm. To help students make the transition from play to quiet attention, build in a round or two designed to slow things down. Make the last round of a game silent. Or, when doing a call-and-response chant such as "Boom Chicka Boom" (find the words and tune online), slowly lower your volume as you do the chant and students will do the same. You could also teach deep breathing, stretching, or a yoga stance as a transition between games and work time.

What's an Energizer?

Energizers are quick, whole-group activities that you can do anywhere, anytime. They can be lively or calming. They don't take much time (three minutes or less), but they can have a big impact on learning and community-building. For example, a short sing-along may help ease the transition from one lesson to the next.

Learn More about Energizers at www.responsiveclassroom.org

Energizers! 88 Quick Movement Activities That Refresh and Refocus by Susan Lattanzi Roser (Northeast Foundation for Children, 2009).

Keep Things Fast-Paced and Fun

Children do best when the pace of games is quick and light. Play or sing a few rounds and then move on. Then do another round later in the day. Also, avoid trying to make sure that each student gets a turn being "it." It's better to play a round unhurriedly and successfully with one or two students in this position. Just be sure you have a transparent and fair system for choosing the "it" person and that all students know they will get a turn at some point when you play the game again. Tell children that not every child will get a turn every game. Remind them that every role in a game is important; if there was just an "it," the game wouldn't work.

Slowly Introduce Partner Games

Partner games such as Go Fish and concentration can provide a fun way for kindergartners to practice academic skills and learn much-needed social skills (turn-taking, being a good sport, and so on). Introduce partner games carefully. Here are some tips:

- **Play partner games as whole-group games first.** Many partner games can easily be adapted for whole-group play. Students can be a "team" and play "against the clock." For example, the class can look around the classroom trying to find as many triangles or capital "T's" as they can in two minutes. Playing as a whole group helps students relax and learn the rules, providing a positive association with the game.

- **Focus on social skills.** When students are ready to play with a partner, use interactive modeling to show how the game looks in the new format. Focus on specific actions students need to take to be successful as a partner—paying attention, following the rules, and taking turns. During this practice phase, assign partners and keep students in the circle so that you can closely monitor them and provide feedback.

■ Introduce competition slowly. Competition can add a lot of stress for children. At first, make partner games noncompetitive, or have the children compete to beat their own record or to beat the clock. For instance: "See how many pairs you and your partner can make together before the timer goes off." Introduce the competition aspect only after the children seem comfortable with this step.

■ Help children understand the concepts of luck and chance. This will help them have fun whether they're winning or losing. Also be sure to teach children what to do and say to show graciousness and good sportsmanship—whether they're losing or winning.

■ Monitor and supervise closely. Even when students are fairly adept at playing a variety of games, continue to monitor game-playing. If a student doesn't follow the rules or treats an opponent unfairly, step in with a redirection or logical consequence.

■ Reinforce teamwork, cooperation, and empathy. Games provide natural opportunities for kindergartners to develop and practice these skills. As students play, move among them and note when they exhibit positive behaviors: "You each said, 'Oh, I'm sorry' when the game didn't go well for the other. That must have made you both feel better." After a game-playing session, ask the class to reflect on key academic and social skills: "I saw people using the word wall when they needed it. Everyone waited patiently for a turn. And you took your turns quickly, too. How did being good partners make the games more fun?"

Sprinkle Songs, Chants, Energizers, and Poems throughout the Day

There's no such thing as too many songs, poems, and chants in kindergarten! Kindergartners can learn so much by chanting, singing, and moving together. These activities support kindergartners' development of reading skills (new vocabulary, sequencing of words, sound-symbol association when written words are introduced, and so on). They help children learn how to follow directions; work together; coordinate thoughts, words, and movements; and more. Singing, chanting, and moving are also quick and powerful ways to build community, reinforce academics, and support

children's growing sense of themselves as capable learners.

You can use songs, chants, energizers, and poems to help kindergartners do transitions and routines,
remember basic content, and just
have fun. Here are some tips:

■ **Invest in some great kindergarten music.** So many talented
people have written and performed music that young children love. As they follow
directions to Ziggy Marley's
"Ziggy Says" or laugh and dance
to Raffi's "Down by the Bay,"
kindergartners will feel the kind
of joy and exuberance that only
good music can inspire.

**Learn More about Games, Songs, and Other
Activities at** www.responsiveclassroom.org

36 Games Kids Love to Play by Adrian Harrison
(Northeast Foundation for Children, 2002).

*99 Activities and Greetings: Great for Morning
Meeting . . . and other meetings, too!* by Melissa
Correa-Connolly (Northeast Foundation for
Children, 2004).

Doing Math in Morning Meeting by Andy
Dousis and Margaret Berry Wilson (Northeast
Foundation for Children, 2010).

Other Resources

*Elementary Teacher's Handbook of Indoor and
Outdoor Games* by Art Kamiya (Parker, 1985).

The Incredible Indoor Games Book by Bob
Gregson (McGraw-Hill, 2004).

*Phonemic Awareness in Young Children:
A Classroom Curriculum* by Marilyn Jager
Adams, Barbara R. Foorman, Ingvar Lund-
berg, and Terri Beeler (Brookes Publishing
Company, 1998).

■ **Try call and response.** Children enjoy call-and-response songs and
chants. These songs and chants also reinforce skills that kindergartners
need to develop, especially careful listening and following directions.
Fun call-and-response songs include "Aroostasha" and "My Sweet Old
Aunt." (To learn these and other songs, see *Energizers! 88 Quick Movement Activities That Refresh and Refocus* by Susan Lattanzi Roser, available
from www.responsiveclassroom.org.) You can use the call-and-response
format for any song or poem: Read a line and then have children repeat
it after you.

■ **Choose songs, poems, and chants with lots of repetition and easy-
to-remember lyrics.** Singing, dancing, and moving are more engaging
to kindergartners when they don't have to learn complicated wording.
Although there's a place for teaching more involved wording, spend most
of your time with repetitive, easy-to-remember songs, poems, and chants
to ensure that all children can participate happily and successfully.

■ **Add movements and instruments.** Make singing and poetry as interactive as possible by adding appropriate movements and letting students tap out the rhythm with rhythm sticks. Invite students to come up with their own movements and lyrics, too.

■ **Show song lyrics or words to poems.** When possible, display the words to songs, chants, and poems. This helps kindergartners make connections between what they say and what they see in print. As the year progresses, make the connection more explicit. Point to words (or let students do so), highlight or change words, or cut up poems and scramble the words so students can unscramble them.

■ **Let students be themselves.** Children need to let their hair down and relax. Times when they're singing, chanting, and reciting are perfect for this. Of course, you want children to stay safe and return to quieter tasks when they finish, but be sure to let them have fun. Allow some silliness. Give individual students (especially those who need a little extra attention) some time to shine. Encourage playfulness by writing funny lyrics to familiar songs with your students or by letting them recite poems or sing songs in different styles (slow motion, fast, in an underwater voice, and so forth).

Special Projects

Kindergartners love the idea of anything "special." Besides being engaging, projects offer unique ways to make connections among curricular areas. During a project on Steve Jenkins's books, for example, students could study an animal of their choice. They could use collage techniques to illustrate that animal and learn about artistic construction. Their collages could become part of a "Guess Who?" display. For a math connection, students could hunt for certain shapes in their classmates' collages. Projects like these help liven up and deepen students' learning. The following guidelines will help you make them successful.

Identify Learning and Curricular Goals

Be careful not to get too caught up in how fun a project would be. I've made that mistake myself. Fun is great, but kindergarten projects should also have clear learning goals. Projects can be used as part of a unit study or as stand-alones. They can be used to support and reinforce learning goals as well as to extend them. They can also help students make connections across the curriculum.

Projects will have a more powerful effect—especially with kindergartners—when they help students learn and practice needed skills. For example, your goals for a project on planting seeds might include having students learn the basics of what plants need and the parts of a plant. You might also identify related math goals (sorting or classifying seeds, measuring plant growth, and so on). So evaluate any project ideas you're considering based on how well they support the learning goals.

Keep Projects Kid-Friendly

It's easy for projects to take on a life of their own or for adults to assume too much of a role. Choose projects that kindergartners will find meaningful and can safely work on with just a little adult help. For instance, if kindergartners are working on a food project, choose recipes that—for the most part—they can make themselves. When children do most of the work, they more fully gain the benefits of such a project—getting practice in following directions, using measurement skills in a real-life setting, and learning to prepare different foods.

When evaluating what projects to do with children, also consider what tasks adults are required to do and compare that with what the children will be doing. Choose projects that are more child-centered.

Sustain Student Interest

Children are capable of intense focus on a project, but they'll lose steam if projects take too long. Choose projects that kindergartners can start and finish within a relatively short time (a few days or a week), such as setting up a small terrarium, making a page for a class book, decorating the class store, or making props for a specific topic for the drama center.

Students will also enjoy projects that last longer if they have opportunities to make new discoveries throughout the project. For example, consider projects such as charting weather changes or plant growth.

Give Students Choices When Possible

Kindergartners have a great deal of curiosity and a strong desire to learn: "Why don't birds fall down from the sky?" "What makes the wind?" Build upon these qualities by offering kindergartners as much say in and owner-ship of projects as you can.

When beginning a unit on weather, for instance, let students generate their own questions. Incorporate these questions into lessons or help students research the answers as part of their project work. Or, at the end of the unit, let students choose from several different ways to demonstrate a key piece of learning. Some might want to create a picture book. Others might want to make a poster or similar display. Such choices keep kindergartners more motivated about their learning.

For more ideas about projects, see "Class Celebrations" on pages 77–81.

Field Trips

For children, probably nothing is as exciting as a field trip outside of school. They'll eagerly anticipate going to the local fire station or a nearby park. These trips can deepen students' learning. But kindergartners may also be fearful of field trips since they have to leave the safety of the classroom.

Field trips can be tricky ventures for kindergarten teachers, too. Recall the advice I gave in Chapter 2, "Schedules and Routines," pages 37–63, about taking into consideration kindergartners' developmental needs as you plan the day and teach expected behaviors. That advice applies even more to field trips! You'll want to plan each field trip carefully, thinking through every detail, and do some thoughtful teaching before (and after) each one. Doing so will help students know what's expected and feel as secure on the trip as they do at school.

Start Small

Kindergartners can develop the skills they'll need and gain confidence by "practicing" going on field trips. Take your students on a field trip within school (to the cafeteria or school office) or outside but still on school grounds (for a tree observation or tour of the play structures). Treat these outings like a real field trip. Beforehand, share expectations and learning goals (such as using the five senses to observe trees). During the outing,

Short on Field Trip Funds?

Consider these alternatives:

- **Have a field trip come to you.** Invite local organizations (an animal shelter for instance) to present at school.

- **Walking field trips.** Visit the local police station or a business. If you are not close to any "site," take your class on some other purposeful outdoor expedition.

- **Museum kits.** Several museums, such as the Boston Children's Museum, offer teaching kits for classroom use. You may have to pay a shipping fee, but the cost is much less than for a bus trip.

- **Virtual field trips.** Many websites such as those for the Smithsonian Institutes (www.si.edu) and the San Diego Zoo (www.sandiegozoo.org) have webpages for children. Ask a technology expert at school about setting up a simulation or other online experience.

Remember to plan learning goals for these activities.

have tasks for students to accomplish (such as drawing one thing they observed about the tree by using their sense of sight). Afterward, have students reflect on what they learned (such as by sharing and talking about their pictures).

As the year progresses, slowly add in more complex field trips. For example, after exploring the school yard, go to a neighborhood park or to a local business before planning a really big field trip—such as one that will require the children to ride on a bus.

When you do plan a big trip, familiarize yourself with the site in advance. For example, you'll want to know where bathrooms are located and where you can eat lunch or a snack. If possible, try to visit the site beforehand and learn more about it online.

Plan for Active Learning

The same principle for all kindergarten activities holds true for field trips—make sure learning is active and interactive. Children need to move, do things, and talk when on trips. If possible, choose sites that have active learning built in (for example, museums with interactive exhibits, parks where children can touch things, and businesses where they can try an actual work task, such as decorating cookies at a bakery).

If the destination doesn't have active learning built in, add it in yourself. Set up a scavenger hunt (using pictures for nonreaders) or give each child a blank book for sketching or taking notes (using simple blank books made by folding and stapling together a few sheets of paper). Also, build in "learning rest stops." Have students stop every fifteen to twenty minutes to do some sort of engaging learning activity (such as sharing an observation) as a whole group, in small groups, or with a partner.

Have Sufficient Adult Supervision

For field trips off school grounds, enlist adults to help make sure the children stick together and don't wander off. Ideally, you'll want to have at least one adult for each small group of kindergartners. Adult volunteers can also help supervise learning tasks that you've assigned to students, accompany children to the bathroom, organize food and water (if needed), and assist with any emergencies that arise. Be sure to provide adult volunteers with guidelines about what to expect and how best to help (see "Involving Parents in Events and Activities" in Chapter 5, pages 131–134).

Assign Students to Small Groups or Pairs Before Leaving School

Field trips with kindergartners will go more smoothly when you think through every detail, including how to pair up and then group students. Start by assigning buddies for every student. Pair up children who get along in the classroom but are not necessarily close friends so children get to know one another better.

Before the trip, talk about and practice ways buddies can help each other (making sure your buddy stays with you, helping if he gets hurt, and so on). Then put pairs of buddies together to form small groups. Assign adults so that each adult supervises one group of no more than four students. If you have students with behavior challenges, place them in your own small group.

Practice Beforehand

Children need guidance about what they'll be doing on the field trip and what the behavioral expectations will be. Remind children that familiar routines and rules (such as the signal for attention and the lining-up routine) will still be used. Before the trip, reinforce these by practicing them during a "pretend" field trip. Remember to also use interactive modeling to teach field trip routines and behaviors. For example:

- **Practice getting there.** If walking, model and practice how students should walk (for example, in a line with their buddy), how fast to walk, and when and how to stop. If going by bus, set up chairs in the classroom like seats on a bus. Practice following bus rules and riding on the bus together.

- **Practice being there.** Model how to sit and listen when the docent or other field trip guide talks (tie this practice to how students listen in the classroom). Be sure to practice the scavenger hunt, touching objects, and other active learning activities for the trip. Kindergartners also need to practice how to use manners on field trips (for example, thanking the host and parent volunteers).

- **Practice having another adult "in charge."** Depending on whether you have had other adults help in the classroom, you may need to practice (with a colleague or adult volunteer) what it looks and sounds like to have an adult other than yourself lead a group of children.

- **Practice asking appropriate questions.** Often, hosts of field trips turn and say to kindergartners, "Do you have any questions?" Kindergartners will have plenty of questions and things to say. However, their responses might not be what the host (or you) expected! Model and practice what is and is not a question and the sorts of questions that would interest everyone.

See Chapter 2, "Schedules and Routines," pages 43–51, for a full explanation of interactive modeling.

Use Familiar Routines and Procedures

On field trips, stick as closely as you can to the routines and procedures you have established for the classroom. Doing so will help children feel more secure and confident. For instance, if students routinely use a nonverbal signal to request bathroom permission, teach that to the adults who will be working with them. This way, students won't have to learn a new signal. Likewise, use the same signals for quiet attention. If you expect children to follow certain rules at school, such as keeping their hands to themselves, hold them to these same high standards while on the field trip.

Be Prepared for Some Changes in Behavior

Even with the best preparation, field trips can create anxiety or other reactions in some children—and these reactions may manifest themselves in changed behaviors. Some kindergartners test limits as they try to figure out who is in charge. Still others cry more readily or argue with friends about seemingly trivial matters. Often, kindergartners experience a tremendous surge of energy at the beginning of the field trip but are really lagging at the end.

To help kindergarteners with field trip behavior:

■ **Be clear about expectations.** If you have classroom rules, make sure students know how those apply during field trips. Be specific about what positive behaviors you expect to see on the field trip. Brainstorm with children how they can maintain these positive behaviors. Reassure them that you will be there to support them, just as you do in the classroom.

■ **Help get students back on track as soon as possible.** Kindergartners thrive on predictability. They'll feel more comfortable on field trips if you react to misbehavior just as you would at school. At the earliest sign of misbehavior, redirect them with clear language ("Matthew, hands to yourself"), a visual cue (finger to lips for a child who is talking while someone else is speaking), or moving closer to a child and putting a hand on her shoulder.

■ **Follow through with consequences if appropriate.** Should a child's misbehavior escalate, use logical consequences. For instance, a kindergartner having difficulty following directions from another adult could be moved to your group for a while.

■ **Take periodic breaks on field trips lasting longer than an hour.** While you'll want to pack as much learning in as possible, be careful. Kindergartners need you to build in regrouping times. You can stop and sing a song together, do a finger play, or even brainstorm highlights of the trip so far.

■ **Be flexible.** You may have planned for kindergartners to see every exhibit at a museum, but if they seem spent after the fourth one, be ready to modify your plans.

Be Prepared for Bathroom Needs and Emergencies

Most field trips go smoothly, but be prepared for the unexpected. Take a cell phone, a basic first-aid kit, and some hand wipes. Remember to check that your destination has bathrooms for students to use. If you're going on a long bus ride, have everyone use the bathroom before leaving school. Then, when you first arrive at the site, again have everyone use the bathroom and make sure that adults accompany them.

Remind adult volunteers to take students to the bathroom as soon as they express a need. With a little luck, these precautions will prevent accidents, but bring some extra clothes and a plastic bag, just in case (see "Bathroom Routines" on pages 54–55).

Think about Food and Water Needs

Children do best on a field trip when they are well-fed and hydrated. You may want to let them have a snack and drink before leaving school. If a field trip is going to last more than an hour, plan for a quick snack and drink at the field trip site, too. Stopping to eat and drink will not only help kindergartners maintain their energy level but will give them a nice break as well.

If the class is going to miss their regularly scheduled lunch, here are some ways to have lunch on the field trip:

- **Collect everyone's lunches before you leave.** Make sure children's names are on their lunches. For students who get lunch from the cafeteria, have their field trip lunches delivered to you or allow yourself time to pick them up. Place all lunches in one or two large shopping bags or boxes.

- **Plan where students will eat.** Check whether the location has tables where children can eat. If not, see if you can get some cloth or paper tablecloths (or blankets) to take along and spread out for a picnic-style lunch.

- **Pack hand sanitizer.** Make sure students use it before eating. You may also want to pack some napkins, paper towels, or wipes to help students with spills or food on their hands and faces.

Reflect on Field Trip Learning

Children benefit most when field trips are connected to what they're learning in school—and when you extend that learning after the field trip. For instance, when you're back at school after a trip to a local veterinarian's office, set up an area (or use the drama center) where students can play vet, acting out the jobs they observed. Include stuffed animals for patients, pads and pencils to write orders, strips of cloth for bandages, and books on animal care.

Field trips often inspire kindergarten writers, so build in some natural opportunities for writing (thank-you notes, a class book, captions for photographs, journal entries, and so on). And be sure to continue reading books that help connect their learning to the field trip.

Closing Thoughts

Kindergartners thrive when they experience the joy of daily games, songs, and poems—and the richness of special projects and field trips. Having the chance to sing, play, and learn together in lively, exciting ways strengthens kindergartners' ties to you, to their classmates, and to their learning. Active, engaging times also match kindergartners' physical and emotional needs— and provide an outlet for their energy and enthusiasm. These special times are great reminders that children learn best when they learn in active ways, socially and academically at the same time.

CHAPTER 5

Communicating with Parents

Parents who ask their kindergartner "How was your day?" are often met with the not-so-informative "Good!" Pressed further with "What did you do today?" they learn the equally unhelpful "Not much." Kindergarten parents, who are often struggling to adjust to their child's going off to kindergarten, can find responses like these very frustrating.

Until this point, parents likely had an intimate knowledge of their child's day, whether at home, day care, or preschool. But this year marks a key turning point in both a child's life and a parent's—a time when the child moves from dependency to greater independence. The event is always jolting, even for parents who've been through the process before with an older child. As one parent cried to me when she left her child at the classroom door one morning, "He's not my baby anymore."

Kindergarten parents need to know what's happening at school—and they need a lot more information than their child can provide! They're counting on your help to make this transition year positive. That's why effective communication between kindergarten teachers and parents is so important.

Kindergarten parents want to know what you're teaching, how to interpret an event their child does report, and how to support their child overall. And while kindergarten parents look to you for this information, they have a great deal to offer you as well—most especially, their deep knowledge of their child.

About the Term "Parent"

Students come from a variety of homes with a variety of family structures. Many children are being raised by grandparents, siblings, aunts and uncles, and foster families. All of these people are to be honored for devoting their time, attention, and love to raising children. Coming up with one word that encompasses all these caregivers is challenging. For simplicity's sake, this book uses "parent" to refer to anyone who is the child's primary caregiver.

Strategies for Good Communication

An open channel of communication to and from parents can help a child flourish in kindergarten. It can also help prevent or correct many misunderstandings, both major and minor. Two-way communication requires that we share our knowledge and expertise with parents and invite them to do the same.

What parents share with you about their child can improve your relationship with them and help you teach children more effectively. One year, I taught a boy with severe speech articulation issues. A few days into school, his mother told me that two of his older siblings were deaf. I then understood that he was likely copying their articulation. Later in the year, another child started struggling with behavior a little more than he had previously. I checked in with his parents and found out that his baby brother was teething and waking everyone up during the night. What the parents told me didn't immediately resolve anything, but in both instances, I gained crucial insights into their children's struggles.

Learn More about Working with Families of Different Cultures at www.responsiveclassroom.org

Parents & Teachers Working Together by Carol Davis and Alice Yang (Northeast Foundation for Children, 2005).

Building a relationship with parents does take some work, but it is very rewarding work. Start by projecting a warm and welcoming presence to all families, not just those that reach out to you. Find something positive about their child to mention in every interaction. Understand that although many parents are eager to be involved with their child's teacher and schooling, many others have school-related anxieties that make such involvement stressful. Maintaining an open, empathetic demeanor will be your key to success in working with *all* parents. Here are some more ideas to help you:

Start Reaching Out Early—with Positives!

Many kindergarten parents are waiting to hear from you before they even know who you are. They want to know who their child's kindergarten teacher will be, what you will be like, and what the year will offer. So

reach out to parents and children as soon as you receive your class list. As the school year progresses, continue to reach out while focusing on the positives.

Your communications don't have to be too involved. Even a quick note home can mean a great deal to parents: "Ali has such an interest in words. The other day, she asked me what 'nocturnal' meant. She is really going to love our unit on animals coming up next month." Sharing the positives you see with parents lets them know that you appreciate their child, which will help them feel more comfortable sharing information with you. Of course, there may be occasions when you have less-than-positive news to share. But if you've been communicating regularly with parents about successes, this news will be easier for them to hear.

You can reach out in many ways:

■ Introductory letter. If possible, send parents a welcoming letter before school starts (see sample on page 114). In this letter, describe yourself briefly. Parents don't need to know your whole life story—just enough to feel some initial comfort with you. Give them some basic information about what kindergarten will be like. If you can, invite them to visit the classroom before the start of school. Some kindergarten parents will be quite anxious to talk with you, so let them know how best to contact you. If you don't have time to send out a letter before school starts, have it ready to go home with students on their first day.

I also often include a short survey for parents to fill out. This is where I ask for contact information and brief information on:

   ❖ Siblings and their ages

   ❖ Pets or special stuffed animals

   ❖ Hobbies or special interests

   ❖ What parents see as their child's strengths

Sample Letter to Parents

Dear Parents and Caregivers,

I am writing to give you a little information about myself and what kindergarten will be like. I moved to California with my dog of 12 years, Mudge, two years ago when I married my husband, Andy. This is my second year teaching kindergarten and my fifteenth year of teaching.

I'm very excited to be teaching your children this year. Socially, they will develop more self-control and learn how to make and keep friends. Academically, they will be learning letters and letter sounds and putting those together to read words. They'll work on reading simple texts and learn about writing as a way to express themselves. They'll also learn to count objects, how numbers relate to each other, simple addition and subtraction, and the names of basic shapes.

Early in the year, we'll explore friendship. We'll read some great children's books about what it means to be a friend. Later in the year, we'll explore animals. We'll look at how to classify animals, investigate where different types of animals live, and read stories about the amazing things animals can do. In the spring, we'll examine plant life. We'll plant our own seeds, go on nature walks, and learn the basics of how plants grow.

Our first order of business will be getting used to school routines and getting to know each other. To start this process, I invite you and your child to come in to meet me and see what the classroom is like on _____ from _____ to _____ p.m. This visit usually helps most children make a smooth transition to kindergarten. Of course, some children may get a little more anxious as school nears. If your child has some extra anxiety, try not to worry—we'll work together to help him or her adjust to school.

I'd love to get to know you and your child, so I've attached a short survey for you to fill out. Please bring it with you during the visiting time. If you can't make that time, please return the survey with your child on the first day of school.

If you'd like to be in touch before then, please call (xxx-xxx-xxxx) any day before 8 p.m. or email me (ms_wilson@school.org) anytime. I look forward to meeting you.

❖ What parents would like their child to accomplish in kindergarten

❖ Anything else parents think would be helpful for me to know

From these surveys, I get insights about students and a picture of their family life, all of which help me teach them more effectively.

■ **Informal classroom visits.** Many kindergartners are nervous about beginning the school year. It helps immensely if they can come see the classroom and meet you before the formal start of school. Be welcoming, open, and positive both to parents and children. Have a place where children can do something active, such as build with blocks, do puzzles, draw, or work with math manipulatives. But to avoid overwhelming children, don't have too many activities or supplies.

■ **Phone calls and email.** Once the school year has started, connect with parents as soon and as often as you can. Chat briefly during drop-off or pick-up times, call on the phone, or email them. (For example, schedule a certain number of families to call or email each day until you work through your class list.) Be positive when making these connections: "Tonya has adjusted well to kindergarten. She is very outgoing and has been playing with other students in the class. She's especially loved playing with class-

---

Helping Students Who Cry or Run Away

It is not unusual for kindergartners to cry during the first few days of school. Here are some ideas to help them and their parents with this challenge:

■ Gently encourage the parent to leave the class quietly. Most children will calm down once their parent has left.

■ Hold the child's hand or sit next to him or her for a few minutes. When parents see you comforting their child, it's easier for them to leave.

■ After a few minutes have passed, help the child focus on something else (a classmate, a favorite book, or an activity).

■ If the child needs longer to calm down, offer a limited choice: "You can sit beside me or you can sit at your table and draw quietly. Which do you think would help most?"

More rarely, a kindergartner may try to run out of the classroom. If this happens, ask a colleague for help or ask the parent to stay until you both are reasonably sure the child will be safe.

If these behaviors occur more often or become more intense, work with parents, administrators, and support staff to find possible solutions.

mates on the swings at recess. What are you hearing about kindergarten at home?"

■ Formal open house ("Parents' Night"). Most kindergarten parents are eager to attend an open house. Make the most of their eagerness by presenting information concisely and concretely. Walk parents through a typical day in kindergarten (using photos of their children to show "a day in the life" can be very powerful). Outline what students will be learning socially and academically throughout the year. Let parents know how to support their children in these areas at home. Display examples of all students' work. Also leave time for questions. (If parents ask questions that pertain to only their child or a few children, let those parents know that you'd be happy to schedule a separate time to talk.)

■ Website. A class website can be a helpful way to keep parents up-to-date and provide learning tips. Parents will most likely visit the site if content changes frequently and includes practical information such as a class calendar, references to resources, and book lists. But before putting the effort into a site, investigate how many students' parents have Internet access. (Be sure to follow your school's or district's guidelines for the use of websites.)

Plan the First Day

Many schools have an official policy for the first day of kindergarten. If yours does not, you'll need to plan for the day and let parents know what to expect. Many parents like to bring their children to the classroom on the first day.

Emailing Parents

In general, serious or confidential matters are best discussed in person, by phone, or in a paper-and-envelope letter. But email can be great for quick notes about day-to-day classroom life. A few things to consider:

■ **Know if parents can—and want to— use email.** At the fall open house, invite parents to sign up to receive email from you if they'd like. Tell them you'll also be communicating in other ways. Judge by the number of sign-ups whether to use email regularly.

■ **Keep the volume of messages manageable by mixing in other ways of communicating.** Most parents rely less on email once they know you'll be sharing news in various ways.

■ **Follow guidelines.** Check whether your school, district, or parent organization has guidelines for emailing families.

116

Letting them do so—and letting them spend a few minutes in the class—can help them and their child feel better about the day. However, let parents know that they should leave fairly quickly because you need to start forming a community of learners. Also, children can pick up on any parental anxiety or sadness, so ask parents to be upbeat when they say good-bye.

Listen

As teachers, we tend to have little time and a lot to say, so truly listening to parents can be challenging. But listening will convey your respect to parents, foster a genuine home-school partnership, and help you learn important information about children and their families.

When parents are talking, refrain from commenting or questioning them right away. Instead, nod or otherwise communicate that you're still listening ("mm-hmm"). If you need clarification or more information, avoid pointed questions, such as "Toby seems perfectly happy to me at school; what is he saying is a problem?" Such questions tend to limit the amount of information you receive and may lead parents to become defensive. Instead, try more open-ended questions, such as "What are some parts of our day that seem particularly challenging or upsetting for Toby?"

Remember that parents have as much to offer you as you do them, so structure your conversations accordingly: Listen, keep an open mind, and ask questions that lead to more, not less, openness.

Empathize

Parents may worry a great deal when their kindergartner is having a problem—whether big or small—in school. When my nephew was in kindergarten, his

Do Parents Have Literacy or Language Issues?

Be on the lookout for indications that students' parents have difficulty reading (in any of the languages used for written communications from school). If they do, avoid overrelying on written information. Look for other ways to communicate, such as phone calls or recorded messages that parents can call in to receive.

117

Communicate With Students, Too!

Because every student needs to feel seen and heard, an occasional note to a student placed in her or his folder or backpack can have a powerful effect.

Dear Juan,

I saw you help Andru when he fell down today. I also saw you help Mr. Johnson when he dropped his papers. I bet both of them felt very special that someone cared.

Although kindergartners will likely need their parents' help to read these notes, they'll still feel special that you wrote just to them.

teacher contacted my sister every time there was a discipline problem. My sister dreaded the teacher's notes and phone calls, primarily because she wasn't sure what to do for my nephew and didn't know quite how (or if) she should ask for help. At some point, I'm sure her frustration leaked out in conversations with the teacher.

As teachers, we can't take that kind of reaction personally. Instead, when parents seem upset with us, we should presume their positive intentions, look for a way to help, and remember that, like teaching, parenting is not an easy job.

Seek Common Ground

Most parents appreciate learning about problems earlier rather than later, so when you have less-than-positive news to share, don't put it off. When a problem is small, it's easier to address. Also, parents won't be surprised if you need to do more involved problem-solving with them at a later time.

Be clear why you are sharing the news. Is it just an FYI? Or do you want parents to do something, and if so, what? If parents disagree with your assessment, don't try to argue your point. Instead, propose an alternative approach that is mutually agreeable.

For example: "This week, Brendan had some difficulties sharing math materials. One time, he grabbed a pattern block from a friend. Another time, he wouldn't let his partner roll the dice in their math game." If the parent says, "That doesn't sound like Brendan; he always shares with his sister at home," propose a solution that builds on this positive behavior: "Let's both talk to him about sharing and let him know that just as he shares with his sister, he needs to share with his classmates. You could also borrow some math materials and let him play school at home with his sister."

Communicate Regularly and Consistently

The more consistent your communication with families, the better your relationship with them will be. If you use a weekly class newsletter or email, send it out the same day each week. If you have a class website, update it on a regular schedule. If you want individual contact with families through phone calls, notes, or emails, set up a manageable schedule for yourself. Of course, events or issues will likely arise that prompt you to communicate right away. Still, if parents know they'll hear from you regularly, they'll trust you more and feel more secure about their child in school.

When parents express concerns during the year, use your regular communication setup to reassure and guide them. (See "Special Concerns of Kindergarten Parents" on page 122.) Let parents know they are not alone, explain what you're doing about these issues at school, and suggest practical strategies for them to try at home. On page 120, there's an example of a note you might send to parents if they express concerns about kindergartners' spelling.

Share Information about Child Development

Most parents crave information about how their child is developing compared with other kindergartners. Rather than making comparisons, though, stress how each child's developmental path is unique and present parents with information about overall child development. Sharing some of the common traits and characteristics of this age (as outlined in the beginning of this book, pages 4–10) can help parents put their child's growth in better perspective. It can also give them some ideas about what to try at home to help their child learn and grow.

Parents might especially benefit from understanding these points about kindergartners' growth and development:

■ **Children develop at different rates.** Human development is complex, and no two children will follow the same developmental path. For example, many kindergartners care a great deal about what their parents and teachers think, but others may be more independent or more concerned about their friends' opinions.

Sample Note to Parents

Concerned about Spelling?

I enjoyed talking with you at the recent parent-teacher conferences. I want to take a minute to address a common question I heard about spelling.

Many parents are concerned that their child is misspelling words. For instance, a kindergartner might spell "school" as "skol" or "store" as "str." I want to assure you that using "temporary spelling" is very common. It's a way for kindergartners to write while they're still developing writing skills. At this point, most kindergartners have learned exact spellings for only a few words.

To help them with their spelling, I'm teaching them to sound out words as they write. This way, they can write more interesting pieces that will help them develop voices as writers and a love of writing.

Let's imagine that a student wrote, "I wnt to the prc. I had a ras wit my dad, an I wun." (Translation: I went to the park. I had a race with my dad, and I won.") Using temporary spelling allowed the child to use a lot of different words and include details and action.

When you read a piece of writing by your child, here's how to support his or her learning at school:

- If you're not sure what the piece says, ask your child to read it aloud.

- Look for the positives. Be specific. For example, "That's a nice detail about having a race."

- Look for correctly spelled words and tell your child you noticed. Remember, though, to focus most on the actual story, not just the way words are spelled.

When your child writes at home, help him or her sound out words (for instance, for "bump," say "What sound do you hear first?" and emphasize the *b* sound). Or help your child look for an easy place to find the word (for example, look for the word "corn" on a cereal box). Avoid spelling every word for your child. That can make children too concerned about spelling and cause them to lose interest in writing.

Thank you for supporting your child's learning! As always, please let me know if you have any questions.

■ **Different aspects of development occur at different rates.** A kindergartner might appear quite advanced in terms of language (for instance, using certain abstract words with ease). That same child, however, might find social situations challenging and revert to "younger" behaviors (such as hitting people when upset). There is no one path along which every child travels.

■ **Children will change as the year progresses.** During the school year, kindergartners may change dramatically in many ways. Toward the end of the year, many may have more fully developed fine motor abilities, leading to better printing and more detailed drawings. Some may also develop a more sophisticated understanding of language.

■ **Growth often happens in fits and starts.** Children may experience great bursts of growth, followed by quieter periods and sometimes by revisiting behaviors from earlier stages. Toward the end of kindergarten, some children might exhibit the "older" behavior of testing limits more. Others might revert to "younger" behaviors that parents thought were over, such as hitting or pushing when upset instead of responding verbally.

■ **Kindergartners may be rigid in their thinking or perspectives.** They often have trouble seeing more than one way to do something or understanding another's viewpoint. Give parents tips for helping their children become more open to other ideas and more empathetic to others. For example, encourage them to read books together that foster multiple perspectives, such as *Seven Blind Mice* by Ed Young or *Duck! Rabbit!* by Amy Krouse Rosenthal and Tom Lichtenheld.

Child Development Resources for Parents at www.responsiveclassroom.org

Yardsticks: Children in the Classroom Ages 4–14, 3rd ed., by Chip Wood (Northeast Foundation for Children, 2007), or the child development pamphlets based on this book.

Another resource:

How To Talk So Kids Will Listen and Listen So Kids Will Talk by Adele Faber and Elaine Mazlish (Harper, 1999).

■ **Many kindergartners thrive on knowing exactly what is expected of them.** Explain to parents that building predictable routines into the schedule at school, being explicit about behavior expectations, and showing children exactly how to do school tasks are ways that we help students feel comfortable in kindergarten—and begin to learn self-control and responsibility. Parents can especially benefit from knowing how children are learning about self-control and other expected behaviors and routines at school.

Invite Parents to Get Involved

Welcome parents into the classroom—it's a powerful way to build connections with families. Parents often wonder about what happens at school, so invite them to observe for a time. Many also want to help in the classroom, so give them opportunities to do so and be sure to provide guidance on how they can be most helpful. (For more on having parents in the classroom, see "Involving Parents in Events and Activities" on page 131.)

Special Concerns of Kindergarten Parents

Knowing some common worries that kindergarten parents have will help you address their concerns and provide them with practical tips for use at home.

Reading

Some parents push their children to make fast progress with reading (for example, by having them read chapter books before they're ready). Others may not know how to support the development of reading skills or they may be struggling with literacy issues themselves. Help parents see that the development of reading skills differs for every child.

Also be prepared to offer all parents practical advice about what to do at home to support their child's development of reading skills. For example, suggest that they:

■ **Read aloud to children.** Tell parents that reading aloud to children is one of the primary ways to support kindergartners' growth as readers and to foster a love of reading. Encourage parents to read aloud daily, to choose a variety of books, and to talk with their children about what they read.

Reading Resources for Parents:

■ *The Read-Aloud Handbook* by Jim Trelease

■ *Reading Magic: Why Reading Aloud to Our Children Will Change Their Lives Forever* by Mem Fox

■ *What to Read When: The Books and Stories to Read with Your Child—and All the Best Times to Read Them* by Pam Allyn

Many reading series also have handouts for parents. Search the Internet for additional resources, or visit WWW.READINGROCKETS.ORG and WWW.RIF.ORG.

■ **Have regular conversations with their child.** Let parents know of the importance of talking with their child—for example, at meal times. These parent-child conversations can help children develop their language and reading skills.

■ **Talk about the importance of reading.** Encourage parents to talk with their children about why they read (reading food labels and recipes to prepare healthy meals, reading the newspaper for community news, and so on).

■ **Make learning to read a positive experience.** If children begin to read to parents (instead of the other way around), give parents tips for keeping reading at home positive. For example, help parents choose books that are appropriate for their child. Remind parents to be patient when their child tries to sound out or determine the meaning of a new word. Tell parents that another way children learn to read is by "reading" a simple, familiar text that they've memorized.

■ **Have a wide variety of books available.** Let children and parents check out books from your classroom. Or make "book bags" for children to take home. Encourage parents to take their child to the public library and get a library card. Tell parents about the value of giving children access to many different types of books.

Other Academic Concerns

Parents often ask a lot of questions about academics throughout kindergarten since it's their child's first "academic" year. Some things they may ask about include:

■ **Letter and number reversals.**
Many parents worry when they see their children writing letters or numbers backwards. Unless you see other issues that concern you, reassure parents that kindergartners commonly reverse letters and numbers and that they'll usually grow out of this phase with time and practice.

■ **Misspellings.** Explain why it's OK for kindergartners to misspell words: Doing so helps them write more fluidly and develop other writing skills. Give parents concrete advice about how to respond positively to their child's writing (see "Concerned about Spelling?" on page 120).

■ **"How can I supplement what my child learns at school?"** Many parents want to support their children's academic development at home but need help to do so. Discourage parents from purchasing workbooks. Instead, give them ideas for making learning fun and related to real life: play store or a board game together; let children count change when out shopping; help children make a simple grocery list or write a short note to a relative; create a memory book by taking photographs and writing captions together. Remind parents of the importance of engaging in thoughtful conversations throughout the day.

Social Issues

Sometimes kindergarten parents will bring up concerns about other children in the class. Their concerns are often about what others may be "doing to" their child or about their child's social abilities. For example, a parent might tell you that their child wants to play with another student but doesn't know how to ask. Or a parent relays that a group of kindergartners won't let their child play with them.

Here are some strategies for handling parents' concerns about social issues:

- **Help parents describe specific situations.** Often, parents, though well intentioned, present their concerns about other children in judgmental language: "Cara says that Alfonso is mean." Help parents move away from this unhelpful language so that you can get a clearer picture of what is happening: "What exactly did Cara say that Alfonso has done?" If parents hesitate, explain why specifics help: "Sometimes children use 'mean' in lots of different ways. I'm trying to get a better sense of what actually happened."

- **Preserve confidentiality.** In responding to parents' concerns about other children, refrain from offering private information or your opinions about these children. Instead, reassure parents that you'll monitor the situation. Advise parents how they can support their child at home. Sometimes serious situations arise, so keep school leaders informed, seek their expertise, and be sure to follow school and district guidelines.

- **Encourage parents to have their children talk directly with you.** When children speak with you (versus when parents act as messengers), you'll have a better sense of how to help. Be open to having children express any concerns so they won't be worried about "tattling" or how you'll respond. Children need to feel confident that it's OK to report incidents to you.

- **Keep parents informed about social skills lessons.** Share with parents the social skills you're teaching children, such as how to ask someone to play and what to do if a child hurts someone else. When parents know what you're teaching, they can help reinforce these lessons at home. If you're teaching about independence and responsibility at school, for example, parents can help reinforce those lessons by having their children carry their own school backpack and keep it in a special place at home.

Homework

If you can, avoid giving kindergartners regular homework. It is very hard to find assignments that they can do independently. As a result, kindergarten homework often requires parent help. This can overload already busy parents and lead to other problems. It may also set up a dynamic that can last into the upper grades in which the child is dependent on parents for homework assistance.

In addition, parents may not know how best to help with homework, and battles may result. For instance, a parent may be dissatisfied with the quality of a child's work, causing the child to become defensive: "My teacher told me to do it this way!"

Perhaps most importantly, kindergartners still need lots of time to play and rest. As kindergarten has become more academic in recent years, children have had less time for play and rest at school. Homework cuts down on this key developmental time even further.

If homework is a school requirement, try to make the experience as productive and as positive as possible for both children and parents. Here are some tips:

- Be clear about the purpose of homework. Make sure parents know the purpose and learning objectives for homework. For example, I tell parents that the homework I assign in kindergarten is supposed to be fun, familiar, and possible for children to do on their own. Some parents may still want to help their child review a skill learned in class. If so, provide information about how they might do so.

- Provide clear homework directions. Make directions—and the activities themselves—as simple, straightforward, and obvious as you can so

126

Homework Help at
www.responsiveclassroom.org

"Homework Blues?" *Responsive Classroom Newsletter*, November 2003.

"Homework! Strategies to overcome the struggles and help all students." *Responsive Classroom Newsletter*, November 2000.

"Is Homework Working?" *Responsive Classroom Newsletter*, February 2006.

Another resource:

Rethinking Homework: Best Practices That Support Diverse Needs by Cathy Vatterott (ASCD, 2009).

that children have the greatest chance of being able to manage on their own (and so that parents who want to help can easily understand the assignment as well). When in doubt, ask a friend who isn't a teacher to try out your directions.

■ **Make homework active and hands-on.** Avoid too many pencil-and-paper tasks. For instance, if you want a kindergartner to learn letters, send home letter cards with game instructions. Or give children scavenger hunt instructions for certain letters.

■ **Provide choice.** All of us like having a say in our work and kindergartners are no different. For example, have the same learning goal—practice these five sight words—but provide choices for how to do that: (1) play a certain computer game; (2) play Go Fish or another memory game with a parent; (3) write or memorize a song that contains the words; or (4) make movements or chants for each word.

■ **Keep homework short.** Plan homework assignments that take no longer than ten to fifteen minutes. Share these time guidelines with parents.

■ **Provide advice for homework struggles.** Homework can be challenging for parents and children if children are unsure about the assignment, get stuck, or just cannot finish it that night. Let parents and children know what to do if children are struggling with homework. For example:

   ❖ Call you at home.

   ❖ Write you a note.

   ❖ Use a "homework pass" (if they have one from you).

Be sensitive to family difficulties. Don't assume that children's home lives lend themselves to easy homework completion. Many children live in challenging settings or have parents who work long hours or struggle with literacy and other issues. Be flexible about homework. Explore other ways to help a child meet homework objectives (ask an experienced colleague for advice if necessary).

127

Productive Parent-Teacher Conferences

Kindergarten parent-teacher conferences may be the first "evaluative" meeting parents have ever had about their child. It's understandable, then, that many kindergarten parents approach the first conference with anxiety. You want to be candid with parents about what you're seeing in the classroom. At the same time, you want to be empathetic about what these first conferences may mean to them. Make sure you plan for these conferences: Consider each child's strengths as well as challenges, think through what issues are most important, be ready to hear parents' views, and keep an open mind.

Sample 30-Minute Conference

One Teacher's Agenda

Opening conversation (five minutes): Share the plan for the conference and help parents relax. Have a quick, positive, and upbeat story about their child to share, or ask parents some open-ended questions. For instance, if it's the first conference of the year, you might ask, "How is Lindsey feeling about getting up and coming to school every day?" or "On your survey, you noted that Carlos loves to draw. Tell me more about what he likes to do at home." In later conferences, you might inquire about some positive developments parents are seeing in their children or what is going well at home.

Report on behavior progress and concerns (ten minutes): Begin with positives and be as specific as you can in describing what you have seen. If you have areas for concern, share those and invite parents' observations with questions such as "What have you been noticing?" Leave time for any additional ideas or concerns from parents.

Report on academic progress and concerns (ten minutes): Again, it's helpful to start with a child's academic strengths, giving as many specifics as possible. Share your concerns and respond to parents' concerns.

Closing (five minutes): Summarize the conference. Make sure parents have time to ask questions or share any other concerns. Plan to check back in together, if appropriate.

Come Prepared

To start off on the right foot with parent-teacher conferences, prepare for them just as you would a lesson, a presentation, or another school event. Review the common characteristics of kindergartners (see pages 4–10). Organize any data (student work, assessments, and so on) you plan on sharing with parents. Make some specific notes or an outline of what you want to cover for each conference. Otherwise, it'll be easy to get sidetracked.

Highlight the Positives

At least a week before the conference, take notes so you have some specific and positive information about what each child's strengths are, both socially and academically. If you find that you lack specific positives for any child, dedicate some time to observing that child so that by conference time you'll have gathered a few. If you have concerns, keep them in perspective: Kindergartners still have a lot of time to develop as students.

Address Concerns Constructively

If you have concerns to share, follow these guidelines to help parents react constructively:

- ■ **Use neutral, nonjudgmental language.** Parents may feel defensive if they hear observations like this: "Brie does not seem to like school. She just doesn't care about doing her schoolwork." Instead of labeling students, describe specific examples of what you see: "At center time, Brie often has trouble getting started on her work. She spends a lot of time arranging and rearranging her materials. When I check on her, she says she knows what to do and gets started. But when I leave, she stops working." Being specific gives parents a clear picture of their child. It can also help them connect what you see at school with what they see at home.

- ■ **Present just one or two concerns.** Be honest with parents, but prioritize your concerns. Deal with one or at most two related concerns at a time. Parents can easily feel discouraged, overwhelmed, or unnecessarily worried when they hear a long list of concerns, especially in kindergarten. They may also feel that you're being too negative about their child.

■ Have a plan and offer practical ideas. Parents may naturally feel alarmed when you tell them about challenges their child is having. To help reassure parents, tell them what you've been doing to support their child and offer some ideas for how both of you can continue this support. And remember to let parents know of a problem early on so that the conference is not the first time they hear about a significant issue.

Be Prepared for Surprises

Sometimes, despite your best preparation, issues that you know little about or are not ready to address may arise at conferences. When parents raise these issues, refrain from commenting, being defensive, or trying to come up with answers or solutions on the spot. Instead, keep an open mind, listen without interrupting, and encourage parents to describe the issue as specifically as possible. For example, ask: "Who is involved? When has it been happening? How long has it been going on?" Then let parents know you need some time to think about and look into the issue yourself. Check back with parents within a reasonable amount of time.

Follow Up

Send parents thank-you notes or a brief follow-up email (know your school's policy for these follow-ups). If issues that needed further attention came up at the conference, be sure to do whatever you discussed and update parents on your progress.

130

How Worried Should You Be?

Part of teaching kindergarten is assessing whether a child has an academic or social problem that needs intervention. Here are some strategies to try:

■ **Keep detailed notes, data, and assessments.** Collecting specific information over time, such as how focused a child is at work times, can be quite telling. A child who goes from not being able to focus at all during work times to being able to sustain five to ten minutes of work within a month's time is making considerable progress.

■ **Consult with an experienced colleague, learning specialist, or school leader.** Tell them what you've observed. Ask them to share possible causes and interventions.

■ **Work with the child individually.** Sometimes, by sitting down for a private session with a child, we can discover whether he can do a task independently, needs our help, or is unable to do the task at all.

Involving Parents in Events and Activities

To enrich the kindergarten experience for students, offer parents many opportunities to participate in school activities. Parent involvement benefits the parents as well—they gain greater insight into their child's world and feel more connected to their child and to the school. And parent volunteers can help teachers plan special events, complete everyday tasks, and manage other aspects of teaching more efficiently.

To make parent participation as productive as possible, follow these tips:

Set Expectations for Parents

Kindergartners can be very black-and-white thinkers. If parents do things too differently from the way you do them, the children may become confused or even anxious. Also, for their own comfort, parent volunteers need to know what to expect and do while they're at school. Don't assume that parents will know. Tell them about any classroom rules and procedures that would be helpful. Fill them in on general behavior expectations, too.

Set out explicitly what you expect from parents, as in the sample guidelines shown in the box titled "Sample Written Guidelines for Parent Volunteers" on the next page. You may also want to set up a meeting with potential volunteers to go over these guidelines and answer any questions they may have.

Sample Written Guidelines for Parent Volunteers

Thanks for volunteering in our class. It means a great deal to your child and our whole class that you're willing to share your time with us.

Here are some guidelines to help you when you volunteer:

- If you have any questions about what you should be doing in the classroom, please ask me.

- When I ring my chime or raise my hand, it means the students should stop talking and look at me. It helps if other adults in the classroom do the same.

- If you're helping students with a project, try to make sure children do as much of the work as possible, take turns, and help to clean up. If you give out materials, have all students keep hands in their laps and wait until everyone has what they need before beginning to work.

- If you're working with a small group, please follow our class rules by speaking to the children respectfully and calmly.

- Most students love working with a parent volunteer, so things will probably go smoothly. But if you're concerned about a child's behavior, please let me know. Feel free to positively redirect children by telling them briefly what you want them to do. ("Keep your hands to yourself." "Stay close to me." "Quiet voices.") But if any further steps are needed, please let me handle them.

- If a student should have a problem, please protect that child's privacy by not discussing it with others.

Maintain Consistent Discipline

Although it may feel awkward to redirect students or use consequences when parents are present, it's important to stick to your usual discipline approach. Doing so will help students feel safe and continue to be productive. This consistency will also help parents work more smoothly since they won't have to worry so much about handling discipline issues themselves.

Be prepared for changes in the behavior of either the child whose parent is volunteering or other students in the class. Some children have a hard time controlling their enthusiasm when parent volunteers visit the classroom. Others might want to test limits to see if the same rules are in place. As always, be firm and respectful, ready to intervene in a timely and unobtrusive

When Children Misbehave During Family Visits

Situation	What You Might Say or Do
Owen's grandmother is teaching the class a traditional song their family sings. Owen is singing in a silly voice and dancing all around. His grandmother keeps stopping her singing and is clearly getting frustrated.	Move beside Owen and tell him quietly to sit down. Stay beside him until he calms down. Once he's calm, suggest how he can productively help his grandmother (for instance, by pointing to the words of the song on a chart).
Mackenzie's dad is helping make a class book based on *It Looked Like Spilt Milk* by Charles G. Shaw. The children are making paint splatter pictures and writing about them while he helps. Mackenzie is having a hard time waiting for her turn. She keeps getting out of her seat to go over to her dad and ask when it will be her turn.	"Mackenzie, bring your work and come sit beside me. Your dad will let you know when it's your turn."
Sam's mother is helping chaperone a field trip to the zoo. Almost immediately, Sam starts demanding that she buy him a souvenir. She keeps firmly refusing and explaining her reasons. But he keeps asking.	Speak to Sam privately: "Sam, your mother has said 'no.' You need to stop asking her. If you can do that, you can stay in her group. If you think that will be too hard, you can be in my group."

way to get the student back on track. The chart above shows some typical situations and ways you might respond.

Give Parents Nonteaching Roles

Most parents don't have the knowledge, skills, or training to actually teach, such as by leading reading groups or explaining how to do a math assignment. Although some kindergarten teachers have students read to parents, even this assignment can be challenging. To do it well, parents need to know how to respond when students don't know words and what to do if a book proves too difficult for students.

Family Participation Ideas

School Day

- Helping with art, science, or other projects
- Chaperoning field trips
- Helping make books of students' writing
- Sharing special art, language, or other expertise
- Having lunch with their child
- Taking photographs for class books and projects
- Photocopying, stapling, cutting, and doing other tasks
- Helping with scrapbooks or memory books

Evening

- **Reading night or book parties:** Students share projects about books they've read.
- **Writing night:** Families and children write books together (original works or adaptations of children's books).
- **Math night:** Families play a variety of math games to build math skills in a fun way.
- **Art gallery openings:** Families view a display of children's artwork.

Save tasks that involve actual instruction for yourself. Parents can help support kindergartners' academic work in many other ways. For example, parent volunteers can guide a small group in playing an educational game, help organize supplies for projects, be guest readers, or type stories that students dictate to them.

Try to Involve All Parents

Early in my teaching career, I learned the importance of having all parents participate in some way. At Parents' Night, an experienced parent encouraged every parent to volunteer, even those who were not comfortable or did not have time to help in the classroom. She passed around a sign-up sheet that enabled parents to volunteer in a variety of ways—by sending in supplies for a project, by cooking something at home for a special classroom event, or by making decorations for a class celebration or play.

It means so much to students when their parents contribute to class life, and when their classmates know their parents are contributing. All parents have resources or talents that can benefit the class. Tap into these and highlight every family's contributions. For instance, when using napkins a family donated for a class celebration, you could say, "Tina, be sure to tell your parents how much we appreciated these napkins. They really go with our theme!" Or when having students write thank-you notes to those who helped with a special event, be sure to include all those who supported the event, not just the most visible ones.

Closing Thoughts

Kindergarten is a pivotal year in the lives of children and their families, and in many ways you are a kindergarten parent's first and most trusted connection to the school system. Set up strong, two-way channels of communication early in the year to help parents and their children get off to a great start. Keep fostering the family-school relationship with positive and consistent communications throughout the year. When you take the time to encourage and guide parents in supporting their children's learning, you help set students up on a path for success that will last throughout their school career!

Favorite Books, Board Games, and Websites

In this section, I tried to choose some of my favorite books, board games, and websites for kindergartners, but the task was akin to choosing just one snack to bring for a long family car trip. So, as my editor pulled the list from my hands, I had to be reminded again that this list is just a start. I hope your students love some of these as much as mine did.

Read-Aloud Books

Picture Books

Baby Rattlesnake by Lynn Moroney, Te Ata, and Mira Reisberg

Bark, George by Jules Feiffer

The Boss Baby by Marla Frazee

Caps for Sale by Esphyr Slobodkina

Chicken Soup With Rice by Maurice Sendak

Color Zoo by Lois Ehlert

Come Along, Daisy by Jane Simmons

Don't Let the Pigeon Drive the Bus! by Mo Willems

Epossumondas by Coleen Salley, illustrated by Janet Stevens

From Head to Toe by Eric Carle

Hairs/Pelitos by Sandra Cisneros

Hush! A Thai Lullaby by Minfong Ho, illustrated by Holly Meade

In the Small, Small Pond by Denise Fleming

Interrupting Chicken by David Ezra Stein

I Stink! by Kate and Jim McMullan

Joseph Had a Little Overcoat by Simms Taback

Kindergarten Diary by Antoinette Portis

Kitten's First Full Moon by Kevin Henkes

LMNO Peas by Keith Baker

Mary Wore Her Red Dress . . . by Merle Peek

Matthew's Dream by Leo Lionni

Mice Squeak, We Speak by Arnold Shapiro, illustrated by Tomie dePaola

More More More Said the Baby by Vera B. Williams

Picture Books CONTINUED

Muncha! Muncha! Muncha! by Candace Fleming, illustrated by G. Brian Karas

My Friend Rabbit by Eric Rohmann

Owl Babies by Martin Waddell, illustrated by Patrick Benson

Round Is a Mooncake by Roseanne Thong, illustrated by Grace Lin

A Sick Day for Amos McGee by Philip C. Stead, illustrated by Erin E. Stead

Snow by Uri Shulevitz

The Snowy Day by Ezra Jack Keats

Strega Nona by Tomie dePaola

Ten Black Dots by Donald Crews

This Little Chick by John Lawrence

Tippy-Toe Chick, Go! by George Shannon, illustrated by Laura Dronzek

Tortillas and Lullabies/Tortillas y Cancioncitas by Lynn Reiser, illustrated by Corazones Valientes

Two of a Kind by Jacqui Robbins, illustrated by Matt Phelan

Uncle Bobby's Wedding by Sarah S. Brannen

The Very Busy Spider by Eric Carle

Who Took the Farmer's Hat? by Joan L. Nodset, illustrated by Fritz Siebel

World Team by Tim Vyner

Yucky Worms by Vivian French, illustrated by Jessica Ahlberg

138

Chapter Books

Anna Hibiscus by Atinuke

Cowgirl Kate and Cocoa by Erica Silverman, illustrated by Betsy Lewin

George Speaks by Dick King-Smith

Gus and Grandpa and the Two-Wheeled Bike by Claudia Mills, illustrated by Catherine Stock

Ling & Ting: Not Exactly the Same! by Grace Lin

Magic Tree House series by Mary Pope Osborne

Mercy Watson series by Kate DiCamillo

Roscoe Riley Rules #1: Never Glue Your Friends to Chairs by Katherine Applegate, illustrated by Brian Biggs

Toys Go Out: Being the Adventures of a Knowledgeable Stingray, a Toughy Little Buffalo, and Someone Called Plastic by Emily Jenkins, illustrated by Paul O. Zelinsky

Classroom Library Books

All the read-aloud books I listed are great to stock in the classroom library. In addition, consider these favorite books (and don't forget the emergent reader sources mentioned in Chapter 2, page 26):

Fiction (All of these are the name of a series or the first book in a series.)

Biscuit by Alyssa Satin Capucilli, illustrated by Pat Schories

Cat the Cat by Mo Willems

Elephant and Piggie by Mo Willems

Frog and Toad by Arnold Lobel

George and Martha by James Marshall

Henry and Mudge by Cynthia Rylant

Hopscotch Hill School by Valerie Tripp

Little Bear by Else Holmelund Minarik, illustrated by Maurice Sendak

Messy Bessey by Patricia and Frederick McKissack, illustrated by Dana Regan

Robin Hill School by Margaret McNamara, illustrated by Mike Gordon

Poetry

Flicker Flash by Joan Bransfield Graham, illustrated by Nancy Davis

Here's a Little Poem: A Very First Book of Poetry compiled by Jane Yolen and Andrew Fusek Peters, illustrated by Polly Dunbar

Honey, I Love and Other Love Poems by Eloise Greenfield, illustrated by Diane and Leo Dillon

¡Pío Peep! selected by Alma Flor Ada and F. Isabel Campoy, English adaptations by Alice Schertle, illustrated by Viví Escrivá

Popcorn by James Stevenson

Tomie dePaola's Mother Goose by Tomie dePaola

What a Wonderful World by George David Weiss and Bob Thiele, illustrated by Ashley Bryan

Wiggle Giggle Tickle Train by Nora Hilb and Sharon Jennings

Informational Texts and Nonfiction

Abe Lincoln: The Boy Who Loved Books by Kay Winters and Nancy Carpenter (ill.)

All About Frogs by Jim Arnosky

Bread Bread Bread and other books in the *Around the World* series by Ann Morris, photographs by Ken Heyman

Clouds by Anne Rockwell, illustrated by Frané Lessac

How to Clean a Hippopotamus by Steve Jenkins and Robin Page

Moon Bear by Brenda Z. Guiberson, illustrated by Ed Young

My Five Senses by Aliki and other books in the *Let's-Read-and-Find-Out Science Series (Stage 1)*

The Popcorn Book by Tomie dePaola

Red Leaf, Yellow Leaf by Lois Ehlert

The Tiny Seed by Eric Carle

A Tree Is Nice by Janice May Udry, illustrations by Marc Simont

The Watcher: Jane Goodall's Life with the Chimps by Jeanette Winter

Wish: Wishing Traditions Around the World by Roseanne Thong, illustrated by Elisa Kleven

140

To find additional books and authors, talk with other teachers, librarians, parents—
and the children themselves.

Board Games and Puzzles

Candy Land (Hasbro)

Concentration and other memory games

Connect 4 (Hasbro)

Dominoes

Floor Puzzles (Melissa & Doug)

Hi Ho! Cherry-O (Hasbro)

Richard Scarry's Busytown Eye Found It! Game (I Can Do That! Games)

Sequence for Kids (Jax)

Websites

BBC Games ■ WWW.BBC.CO.UK/SCHOOLS/GAMES Contains a variety of interactive games across subject areas.

NCTM Illuminations ■ HTTP://ILLUMINATIONS.NCTM.ORG Offers a variety of activities and lessons for teaching math; based on the NCTM standards.

PBS Kids ■ HTTP://PBSKIDS.ORG Offers a variety of educational, interactive games, many of which are based on well-known characters from children's literature.

Reading A–Z ■ WWW.READINGA-Z.COM Contains resources for teachers, including printable leveled books, phonics lessons and worksheets, and assessment resources. Provides limited access for free; requires subscription for full access.

Roy: Tale of a Singing Zebra ■ WWW.ROYTHEZEBRA.COM Contains a variety of interactive reading games and online books, as well as resources for teachers.

Starfall.com ■ WWW.STARFALL.COM Gives children the opportunity to read, hear, and interact with a variety of books for beginning readers.

ACKNOWLEDGMENTS

The kindergartners I taught were a source of constant inspiration and made me a better teacher. Many thanks to them and to their families for trusting me with their children.

I want to thank my friend Kathi Luster for the help, friendship, and inspiration she provided on a daily basis as she taught kindergarten next door. She is an amazing teacher, and I learned so much from her. Thanks also to Carolyn Cole and Sandra Griessbach, my other two kindergarten colleagues, for all that they shared and did for me.

I had help from many other kindergarten teachers as I worked on this book. My colleague Suzi Sluyter was kind enough to respond at length to my email queries. Suzi embodies all the great qualities of a kindergarten teacher—I was even fortunate enough to watch videos of her teaching while I worked on this book! Candace Baker and Joey Braxton provided laughs, joy, and much information as they shared their insights about kindergarten with me and let me hang out in their classrooms. I also want to thank and acknowledge Mickey Woods, who was my mentor years ago when I student-taught and gave me my first view of a great kindergarten experience.

Robin Smith has been so generous in sharing all her children's literature expertise for this book and for the other *What Every Teacher Needs to Know* books I wrote. Thanks to her and to all of the Newberians for sharing their love of books, laughs, and insights over the years.

As always, I was blessed with the help of great colleagues from NEFC as I worked on this project. Thanks especially to Babs Freeman-Loftis—no words can describe how much her friendship and support mean to me. Alice Yang, Jim Brissette, Elizabeth Nash, and Cathy Hess helped me keep my eye on the big picture and edited my words to better effect. I'd also like to thank Marlynn Clayton and Joan Riordan for their insights and suggestions when reviewing the manuscript. Helen Merena's talents make the book beautiful to behold, and I thank her for that and the kindness she always shows to me personally.

I could never write a book about teaching without thanking my mentors, Kathy Woods and Paula Denton, or my steadfast and generous friend, Lara Webb.

I also want to thank my husband, Andy, who kept me smiling and inspired even when I found teaching kindergarten challenging. And I want to thank my little boy, Matthew, who has given new meaning to the word "joy" in my life and happily let me try out many of the books that I share in the Appendix. My family's constant support always keeps me going. I especially want to thank my sister Judy for her support of my teaching. One telling example of her help was when Judy and a student teacher willingly visited the classroom as "The Stinky Cheese Man!" My niece Kyle deserves special thanks as well. During much of my teaching career, she has helped out in my classrooms in ways too numerous to mention.

Finally, thanks to my parents, the ultimate teachers.

 **Margaret Berry Wilson** is a *Responsive Classroom*® consultant with Northeast Foundation for Children. Margaret has been using the *Responsive Classroom* approach since 1998 and presenting *Responsive Classroom* workshops since 2004. She worked as a classroom teacher in Nashville, Tennessee, for thirteen years and then in San Bernardino, California, for two years.

Margaret is the author of two other books in the *What Every Teacher Needs to Know* series (first grade and second grade), plus *Doing Math in Morning Meeting: 150 Quick Activities That Connect to Your Curriculum* (with co-author Andy Dousis; Northeast Foundation for Children, 2010). She lives in Riverside, California, with her husband, Andy, their adorable son, Matthew, and their aging but perfect dog, Mudge.

About the *Responsive Classroom*® Approach

All of the recommended practices in this book come from or are consistent with the *Responsive Classroom* approach. Developed by classroom teachers and backed by independent research, the *Responsive Classroom* approach emphasizes social, emotional, and academic growth in a strong and safe school community. The goal is to enable optimal student learning. The following are strategies within the *Responsive Classroom* approach, along with resources for learning about each.

All these resources are published by Northeast Foundation for Children and available from WWW.RESPONSIVECLASSROOM.ORG ■ 800-360-6332.

Morning Meeting: Gathering as a whole class each morning to greet one another, share news, and warm up for the day ahead

> *99 Activities and Greetings: Great for Morning Meeting … and other meetings, too!* by Melissa Correa-Connolly. 2004.

> *Doing Math in Morning Meeting: 150 Quick Activities That Connect to Your Curriculum* by Andy Dousis and Margaret Berry Wilson with an introduction by Roxann Kriete. 2010.

> *Morning Meeting Activities in a Responsive Classroom* DVD. 2008.

> *The Morning Meeting Book* by Roxann Kriete with contributions by Lynn Bechtel. 2002.

> *Morning Meeting Greetings in a Responsive Classroom* DVD. 2008.

> *Morning Meeting Messages K–6: 180 Sample Charts from Three Classrooms* by Rosalea S. Fisher, Eric Henry, and Deborah Porter. 2006.

> *Sample Morning Meetings in a Responsive Classroom* DVD and viewing guide. 2009.

Foundation-Setting During the First Weeks of School: Taking time during the critical first weeks of school to establish expectations, routines, a sense of community, and a positive classroom tone

> *The First Six Weeks of School* by Paula Denton and Roxann Kriete. 2000.

> *Guided Discovery in a Responsive Classroom* DVD. 2010.

> *Teaching Children to Care: Classroom Management for Ethical and Academic Growth K–8*, revised ed., by Ruth Sidney Charney. 2002.

Positive Teacher Language: Using words and tone as a tool to promote children's active learning, sense of community, and self-discipline

> *The Power of Our Words: Teacher Language That Helps Children Learn* by Paula Denton, EdD. 2007.

> *Teacher Language in a Responsive Classroom* DVD. 2009.

Rule Creation and Logical Consequences: Helping students create classroom rules to ensure an environment that allows all class members to meet their learning goals; responding to rule-breaking in a way that respects students and restores positive behavior

> *Creating Rules with Students in a Responsive Classroom* DVD. 2007.

> *Rules in School: Teaching Discipline in the Responsive Classroom*, 2nd ed., by Kathryn Brady, Mary Beth Forton, and Deborah Porter. 2011.

Interactive Modeling: Teaching children to notice and internalize expected behaviors through a unique modeling technique

> *Rules in School: Teaching Discipline in the Responsive Classroom*, 2nd ed., by Kathryn Brady, Mary Beth Forton, and Deborah Porter. 2011.

> *Teaching Children to Care: Classroom Management for Ethical and Academic Growth K–8*, revised ed., by Ruth Sidney Charney. 2002.

Classroom Organization: Setting up the physical room in ways that encourage students' independence, cooperation, and productivity

Classroom Spaces That Work by Marlynn K. Clayton with Mary Beth Forton. 2001.

Movement, Games, Songs, and Chants: Sprinkling quick, lively activities throughout the school day to keep students energized, engaged, and alert

16 Songs Kids Love to Sing (book and CD) performed by Pat and Tex LaMountain. 1998.

99 Activities and Greetings: Great for Morning Meeting…and other meetings, too! by Melissa Correa-Connolly. 2004.

Doing Math in Morning Meeting: 150 Quick Activities That Connect to Your Curriculum by Andy Dousis and Margaret Berry Wilson with an introduction by Roxann Kriete. 2010.

Energizers! 88 Quick Movement Activities That Refresh and Refocus, K–6 by Susan Lattanzi Roser. 2009.

Morning Meeting Activities in a Responsive Classroom DVD. 2008.

Solving Behavior Problems with Children: Engaging children in solving their behavior problems so they feel safe, challenged, and invested in changing

Solving Thorny Behavior Problems: How Teachers and Students Can Work Together by Caltha Crowe. 2009.

Sammy and His Behavior Problems: Stories and Strategies from a Teacher's Year by Caltha Crowe. 2010. (Also available as an audiobook.)

Working with Families: Hearing parents' insights and helping them understand the school's teaching approaches

Parents & Teachers Working Together by Carol Davis and Alice Yang. 2005.

About Child Development

Understanding children's development is crucial to teaching them well. To learn more about child development, see the following resources:

Child and Adolescent Development for Educators by Michael Pressley and Christine McCormick. Guilford Press. 2007. This textbook presents understandable explanations of theories and research about child development and suggests ways to apply those theories and research to classroom teaching.

Child Development, 8th ed., by Laura E. Berk. Pearson Education, Inc. 2009. This textbook summarizes the history and current thinking about child development in easy-to-understand prose. The author outlines the major theories and research and provides practical guidance for teachers.

Child Development Guide by the Center for Development of Human Services, SUNY, Buffalo State College. 2002. WWW.BSC-CDHS.ORG/ FOSTERPARENTTRAINING/PDFS/CHILDDEVELGUIDE.PDF. The center presents characteristics of children at each stage of development in an easy-to-use guide for foster parents.

"The Child in the Elementary School" by Frederick C. Howe in *Child Study Journal*, Vol. 23: 4. 1993. The author presents the common characteristics of students at each grade level, identified by observing students and gathering teacher observations.

"How the Brain Learns: Growth Cycles of Brain and Mind" by Kurt W. Fischer and Samuel P. Rose in *Educational Leadership*, Vol. 56: 3, pp. 56–60. November 1998. The authors, who blend the study of child development with neuroscience, summarize their prior work in a format intended for educators. They conclude that "both behavior and the brain change in repeating patterns that seem to involve common growth cycles."

"The Scientist in the Crib: A Conversation with Andrew Meltzoff" by Marcia D'Arcangelo in *Educational Leadership*, Vol. 58: 3, pp. 8–13. November 2000. Written in an interview format, this article dispels myths about child development and explores ways in which research about cognitive development might inform the work of educators.

Yardsticks: Children in the Classroom Ages 4–14, 3rd ed., by Chip Wood. Northeast Foundation for Children. 2007. This highly practical book for teachers and parents offers narratives and easy-to-scan charts of children's common physical, social-emotional, cognitive, and language characteristics at each age from four through fourteen and notes the classroom implications of these characteristics.

Your Child: Emotional, Behavioral, and Cognitive Development from Birth through Preadolescence by AACAP (American Academy of Child and Adolescent Psychiatry) and David Pruitt, MD. Harper Paperbacks. 2000. Intended for parents, this book presents information about children's development and the characteristics of each stage and offers tips for helping children develop appropriately.

Northeast Foundation for Children, Inc., a not-for-profit educational organization, is the developer of the *Responsive Classroom*® approach to teaching. We offer the following for elementary school educators:

PUBLICATIONS AND RESOURCES

- Books, CDs, and DVDs for teachers and school leaders

- Professional development kits for school-based study

- Website with extensive library of free articles: WWW.RESPONSIVECLASSROOM.ORG

- Free quarterly newsletter for elementary educators

- The *Responsive*™ blog, with news, ideas, and advice from and for elementary educators

PROFESSIONAL DEVELOPMENT SERVICES

- Introductory one-day workshops for teachers and administrators

- Week-long institutes offered nationwide each summer and on-site at schools

- Follow-up workshops and on-site consulting services to support implementation

- Development of teacher leaders to support schoolwide implementation

- Resources for site-based study

- National conference for administrators and teacher leaders

FOR DETAILS, CONTACT:

Northeast Foundation for Children, Inc.
85 Avenue A, Suite 204, P.O. Box 718
Turners Falls, Massachusetts 01376-0718

800-360-6332 ■ www.responsiveclassroom.org
info@responsiveclassroom.org